Rescuing Social Capital from Social Democracy

Rescuing Social Capital from Social Democracy

JOHN MEADOWCROFT & MARK PENNINGTON

FOREWORD BY PETER J. BOETTKE

The Institute of Economic Affairs

First published in Great Britain in 2007 by
The Institute of Economic Affairs
2 Lord North Street
Westminster
London SW1P 3LB
in association with Profile Books Ltd

The mission of the Institute of Economic Affairs is to improve public understanding of the fundamental institutions of a free society, by analysing and expounding the role of markets in solving economic and social problems.

ISBN 978 0 255 36592 5

Many IEA publications are translated into languages other than English or are reprinted. Permission to translate or to reprint should be sought from the Director General at the address above.

Typeset in Stone by MacGuru Ltd
info@macguru.org.uk

Printed and bound in Great Britain by Hobbs the Printers

CONTENTS

THE AUTHORS

John Meadowcroft

John Meadowcroft is Lecturer in Public Policy at King's College London. He is the author of *The Ethics of the Market* (Palgrave, 2005), which won an Intercollegiate Studies Institute/Templeton Enterprise Award, co-editor of *The Road to Economic Freedom* (Edward Elgar, 2006) and a Deputy Editor and Book Review Editor of the IEA journal *Economic Affairs*.

Mark Pennington

Mark Pennington is Senior Lecturer in Political Economy at Queen Mary College, London. He is the author of *Planning and the Political Market* (Athlone, 2000), *Liberating the Land* (IEA, 2002), as well as numerous articles in academic journals. In 2006 he became the eleventh recipient of the Atlas Economic Research Foundation award for excellence in the Study of Spontaneous Orders.

FOREWORD

The social and political sciences are prone to fads and fashions. Various philosophies and techniques come to dominate a field for a generation or more until the next new movement is afoot. There is a lot of politics and sociology that explains these swings in what is considered fashionable. In other words, it is not always truth-tracking which drives science, and as a result the development of ideas does not move in a smooth path from falsehood to truth, an upward and onward march from intellectual darkness to enlightenment. Ideas come and go; truths that were once established become forgotten.

Such is the case with the idea of social capital and civil society. During the 1980s and 1990s, on the heels of Robert Putnam's *Making Democracy Work*, the idea of social capital spread throughout the social and political sciences. It almost appeared at one point that one could not write a paper in political science, sociology or even economics without making some use of the concept of social capital.

In *Rescuing Social Capital from Social Democracy*, John Meadowcroft and Mark Pennington examine how the Putnam-inspired use of social capital confuses our understanding of the role of the market in civil society and the positive social capital that is created through commerce. The Putnam research agenda tends to contrast the market with civil society and sees the market economy as undermining the formation of social capital in communities. It is market forces which drive us into the atomistic existence that threatens the future viability of democratic governance. An awakening of civil society is required. We need more civic engagement, more talking to one another: in short, we need more democracy.

But what if markets are one of the most fundamental components of civil society? Hayek has informed his readers that the Greek meaning of the exchange order (the catallaxy) is to bring a stranger into friendship. Voltaire, Montesquieu, Hume and Smith all wrote extensively about the civilising role that commerce plays in social cooperation through reconciling the interests of ethnically and religiously diverse parties. The market is a school of rules, where good behaviour is rewarded, and bad behaviour is penalised. We learn through our experience with markets various habits and values, such as principles of hard work, producing value, honesty in dealings, and promise-keeping. Peter Bauer talked about the move from subsistence to exchange as characterised not only by enhanced material opportunities, but also by a transformation of habits and values on the part of the people: what Tocqueville refers to as 'hearts and minds'.

Besides the confusion over the market, the very nature of a democracy is distorted in the Putnam framework. The democracy that Tocqueville praised in America was a self-governing citizenry, not an endless conducting of town-hall meetings where everyone got a chance to speak their mind and all interests were represented. Instead, politics understood in this way is what kills effective democracy according to Tocqueville. A self-governing citizenry is one of free and responsible individuals. Only a population of self-governing people can make democracy work. In other words, civil society does not enable the state, but limits what the state does by serving as an effective governing mechanism in most walks of life. The state (and its apparatus of compulsion), from this perspective, is restricted to those areas, and only those areas, within which it can operate effectively. Both in terms of scale and scope the state is restrained.

The social democratic interpretation of social capital, on the other hand, argues for a greater role of the state in society, bolstered by 'civil society'. Civil society is contrasted with the market (the nexus of voluntary exchanges). But this use distorts the meaning of civil society from Locke through the Scottish Enlightenment up to thinkers such as F. A. Hayek and Vincent Ostrom.

Rescuing Social Capital from Social Democracy is an outstanding work in both communicating this modern intellectual history of the concept of social capital and critiquing it, but also providing the background history of the concept and the necessary relationship between markets, democratic governance and social cooperation. It is my sincere hope that scholars and students will read this work carefully and come to appreciate the social and cooperative nature of the free market economy. There is no greater force evident in the history of humanity for us to reconcile our differences, and come together to cooperate with one another in peaceful and prosperous ways. Hayek's use of the term 'marvel' to describe the market referred to the technical ability to coordinate the dispersed knowledge in a modern economy, but it could just as well have been invoked to explain the 'marvel' that Voltaire identified so long ago as the great civilising force the market exerts on our violent and frail human character.

PETER J. BOETTKE

Department of Economics,
George Mason University,
Fairfax, Virginia, USA

The views expressed in this monograph are, as in all IEA publications, those of the author and not those of the Institute (which has no corporate view), its managing trustees, Academic Advisory Council members or senior staff.

ACKNOWLEDGEMENTS

We would like to thank Paul Lewis of King's College London and the IEA's two anonymous referees for their comments on an earlier version of this monograph. We would also like to acknowledge the generous support of the Earhart Foundation.

SUMMARY

- Social capital refers to the norms of trust that enable a society to function effectively. A huge cross-disciplinary literature on social capital has arisen, which covers economics, sociology, political science and anthropology.
- Many on 'the left' regard the concept as a magic bullet that, if supplied by governmental institutions, can make political interventions in economic and social life more effective. As such the idea of social capital has been used to justify the 'third way' of social democracy.
- Given its influence, it is important to expose the analytical flaws that have led scholars of social capital to question the role of markets and to support social democratic policy conclusions.
- Many of the institutions of civil society that people point to as having provided social capital historically were exclusive and prevented access to the market by outsiders. For this reason, these institutions may hold back economic development.
- Global expansion of markets has allowed communities that have little in common to become connected by trade, thus leading to the development of a more inclusive form of 'bridging' social capital. People involved in such trading relationships must obey 'thin' moral rules, but may have little in common culturally.

- Brand names, professional organisations, intermediaries and middlemen supply 'bridging' social capital by helping consumers to trust in the products they buy, even across a global economy.
- In a market economy the development of 'bonding' social capital – trust among groups of relatively close knit persons – can co-exist with more impersonal 'bridging' relationships and can provide commercial advantages by reducing search and transaction costs.
- Even if the market 'under-supplies' social capital, the state cannot know how to provide the 'optimal' level. The state cannot anticipate the particular social norms that provide the 'right sort' of social capital.
- Ultimately, if the state attempts to 'build social capital', the amount that is supplied and the form in which it is supplied will be determined by special interest groups, politicians and bureaucrats.
- Governments are no better at 'cultural planning' than they are at economic planning. Democratic politics works best when the state undertakes a limited range of functions and allows markets and civil society to evolve and build their own social capital.

**Rescuing Social Capital from
Social Democracy**

1 INTRODUCTION

The concept of social capital has generated enormous interest in the past decade, such that a search of the *International Bibliography of the Social Sciences* up to April 2007 reveals over two thousand returns. Following the publication of James Coleman's seminal article[1] on the role of social capital in the creation of human capital and Robert Putnam's account of the ability of social capital to promote economic development,[2] hundreds of books and thousands of articles have been published on the subject.

Social capital has generated such interest for two principal reasons. First, it is a concept that has relevance to all the social sciences. Economists, sociologists, political scientists, anthropologists and historians have all engaged with and written on the subject.[3] And second, extraordinary claims have been made for social capital, fuelling the interest of scholars and policymakers alike. Following Putnam, it has been claimed that social capital is a kind of 'magic bullet' that can make public policy initiatives

---

1   Coleman, J. (1988) 'Social capital in the creation of human capital', *American Journal of Sociology*, S94: 95–120.

2   Putnam, R. (1993) *Making Democracy Work*, Princeton, NJ: Princeton University Press.

3   The relevance of social capital to a wide range of academic disciplines has been frequently noted – see, for example, Herreros, F. (2004) *The Problem of Forming Social Capital: Why Trust?*, Basingstoke: Palgrave.

and even democracy itself 'work' more effectively.[4]

For classical liberals who believe in a society characterised by limited government and open markets, social capital is of particular interest because many of the interventionist arguments associated with the 'third way' and the revival of a 'civic republican' version of social democracy make explicit use of the concept. Social democracy is, of course, a broad church which includes a diverse array of policy positions. For present purposes, however, we define it as a political attitude that, while not hostile to markets per se, contends that markets should be 'kept in their place' and supplemented by a host of government interventions that typically exceed those recognised by economists as necessary to counteract examples of 'market failure'.[5]

On the one hand, contemporary social democrats argue that the excessive penetration of markets and market-like processes into public life may undermine the very values that are necessary to sustain a functioning market economy. On the other hand, it is claimed that the failure of previous interventionist experiments owed much to the absence of social capital and that with appropriate public policies to 'build' social capital, collective action problems and other sources of 'government failure' can be resolved. The conviction that government failures may be explained by an absence of social capital and hence can be avoided

4   See, for example, Leigh, A. K., Putnam, R. D. (2002) 'Reviving community: what policy-makers can do to build social capital in Britain and America', *Renewal*, 10(1): 15–20; Blair, T. (2002) 'New Labour and community', *Renewal*, 10(2): 9–14. For a discussion, see Hooghe, M., Stolle, D. (2003) 'Introduction: generating social capital', in Hooghe, M., Stolle, D. (eds) (2003) *Generating Social Capital*, Basingstoke: Palgrave.

5   By this definition there are social democrats in all the major UK political parties. Indeed, in our view social democracy is currently by far and away the majority position across the three main parties.

if this special ingredient is added to the mix leaves the way open for a host of failed policies to be reintroduced if and when it is believed that the appropriate social capital is present.

This paper aims to rescue social capital from the current monopoly over its use exercised by contemporary social democratic theory. It will be argued that, far from being self-devouring, open markets can and do generate the social capital necessary to sustain their own functioning. Second, it will be shown that attempts to 'build social capital' through a programme of 'active' or 'enabling' government may be subject to the very same critiques that undermined support for such intervention in the first place.

The argument is structured in seven parts. Chapter 2 considers the important question of what social capital is and how it should be defined and understood. Chapter 3 sets out the theoretical critique of market liberalism in contemporary social democratic theory. Building on the work of classical liberals both past and present, Chapters 4 and 5 counter this critique by setting out the processes that allow market institutions to sustain themselves without the visible hand of government action. Chapter 6 outlines the second set of social democratic claims – the notion that state-sponsored attempts to build social capital can help avoid examples of 'government failure'. Drawing on insights from both the Austrian and public choice schools of political economy, Chapters 7 and 8 contend that government agents may simply not be in a position to 'plan' the evolution of social capital and that incentives built into the political process may be more likely to reinforce rent-seeking behaviour. The conclusion sets out some classical liberal principles to guide policymakers in the proper application of the social capital concept both at home and abroad.

2 DEFINING SOCIAL CAPITAL

In common with many of the major concepts used by social scientists, social capital may be understood and interpreted in a variety of different ways. A number of core themes may, however, be identified and synthesised to create a workable understanding of what is usually meant by the term.

The phrase social capital was originally coined by the urban anthropologist Jane Jacobs in her study *The Death and Life of Great American Cities*, first published in 1961.[1] Jacobs described the informal networks that existed between different tradespeople, shopkeepers and their customers on particular streets and neighbourhoods as 'a city's irreplaceable social capital'.[2] If a city is to thrive and spontaneously generate wealth and wellbeing, informal networks of communication, trust and reciprocity must be in place among a relatively stable population. It is these networks which Jacobs believed constituted the key ingredients essential to a successful city.

The importance Jacobs attributed to social capital in creating living and self-sustaining cities highlights the first identifiable feature of social capital. Like all capital, social capital is a *resource* that can be put to productive use. According to Coleman, 'social

---

1   Jacobs, J. (1961/1993) *The Death and Life of Great American Cities*, New York: The Modern Library.
2   Ibid., p. 180.

capital is productive, making possible the achievement of certain ends that in its absence would not be possible'.[3]

The second identifiable feature, also implicit in Jacobs's original description, is that social capital can only be present in the relationships *between* people. Social capital is *social* because by definition it cannot be possessed by a lone individual, but requires the presence of others. As Coleman puts it, 'social capital inheres in the structure of relations between actors and among actors'.[4]

At the most basic level of analysis social capital may be said to be present among, for example, a group of machine workers employed in a small factory who enjoy each other's company and encourage one another to work hard, so that the group as a whole is more productive than if each individual worked in isolation without contact with the others.

Jacobs's initial identification of social capital among the seemingly disparate populations of large cities should, however, draw attention to the fact that social capital is often understood to describe relationships between people who are *not* well known to one another or who may be strangers. Social capital has been defined as 'norms of reciprocity and networks of civic engagement',[5] suggesting that it principally describes norms and networks that exist at a societal or community-wide level, rather than the more particularistic relationships among families, friends or work colleagues. Hence, social capital is frequently described as the generalised norms of trust and reciprocity that exist between people who are not well known to one another.

---

3   Coleman (1988) op. cit., p. 98. See also Herreros (2004) op. cit., p. 5.

4   Ibid., p. 98.

5   Putnam (1993) op. cit., p. 167.

Bonding and bridging social capital

Within the above context, Putnam has made an important distinction between *bonding* (or exclusive) social capital and *bridging* (or inclusive) social capital.[6] Bonding social capital describes the cohesion that exists between small groups of similar people, such as family members, close friends and colleagues, and perhaps the members of ethnic or religious groups, while the bridging variety describes the networks that link acquaintances who may be very dissimilar people, such as a businesswoman and her customers. According to Putnam, 'Bonding social capital is good for under-girding specific reciprocity and mobilizing solidarity,' while bridging social capital 'is better for linkage to external assets and for information diffusion'.[7] In other words, bonding social capital ensures a sense of social solidarity within small groups, while bridging social capital links often disparate people and provides information about opportunities outside the small group.

Putnam's distinction between bonding and bridging social capital and his description of the uses of each has strong echoes of Granovetter's work demonstrating the importance of 'weak ties' over 'strong ties'.[8] Granovetter argued that it is the weak ties that exist between acquaintances, rather than the strong ties that exist between friends, which are the most productive. Because small groups of close friends usually possess the same information and know the same people, they tend not to be particularly useful in providing one another with new information or opportunities. By contrast, quite distant acquaintances tend to have different friends

6   Putnam, R. (2000) *Bowling Alone*, New York: Simon and Schuster, pp. 22–3.

7   Ibid., p. 22.

8   Granovetter, M. (1973) 'The strength of weak ties', *American Journal of Sociology*, 78(6):1360–80; Granovetter, M. (1983) 'The strength of weak ties: a network theory revisited', *Sociological Theory*, 1: 201–33.

and contacts and possess different information, which often proves more useful in opening new horizons of opportunity.

Granovetter's study of the discovery of information about employment opportunities, for example, showed that people were more likely to have found out about their present job from an acquaintance – perhaps someone they had met only once or twice before – than from a close friend. Hence, social mobility seems to be more dependent upon a large number of weak ties to people an individual does not know very well, rather than on the strong ties among close friends and colleagues.

It is clear that bonding and bridging social capital perform different but important functions, but it is probably true to say that harmonious societies require the presence of both types of social capital.

Having said that, it is important to note that bonding social capital may also have a 'dark side' which can produce pernicious consequences.[9] The powerful and often exclusive norms of trust and togetherness implied by bonding arrangements are clearly essential to the cohesion of close-knit criminal groups such as the Mafia and the Ku Klux Klan, whose very survival depends upon the loyalty of individual members to the group. Without the existence of such loyalty codes, criminal organisations of this nature could not function. The existence of bonding social capital, then, may not always have positive consequences. In the absence of bridging social capital, however, a large-scale society could not function effectively. People would be less able to cooperate on the tasks required to produce goods and services and would not trust one another to honour contracts.

---

9   Putnam (2000) op. cit., ch. 22. See also Levi, M. (1996) 'Social and unsocial capital', *Politics and Society*, 24: 52.

3 SOCIAL CAPITAL, SOCIAL DEMOCRACY AND THE CRITIQUE OF LIBERAL MARKETS

The operation of a market economy, which involves multiple exchanges between decentralised individuals and organisations, depends in large part upon the existence of trust between market participants. In order for individuals to enter into contracts with others they must trust those people to honour these arrangements. Critics of liberal markets, however, maintain that an externality resulting from the operation of market forces is the erosion of such trust: markets are alleged to be 'self-devouring' processes that consume their own foundations if left unrestricted. Plant, for example, argues that

> [I]n order to work effectively the market requires certain moral attitudes on the part of those involved, and ... there is some danger of these moral underpinnings being disturbed by markets themselves, thereby striking at the roots of their own effectiveness and efficiency.[1]

According to this view, social capital is understood as a form of trust that is created outside the marketplace and is consumed but not replenished by commercial relationships. Newton, for example, defines social capital in terms of the collective goods and services produced in the voluntary sector, outside the realm of the

1 Plant, R. (1999) 'The moral boundaries of markets', in Norman, R. (ed.) (1999) *Ethics and the Market*, Aldershot: Ashgate, p. 10.

family, market or state.[2] Similarly, Ciscel and Heath argue that the creation of social capital is a positive externality of the non-market provision of goods and services because such voluntary relationships bind people together as communities and families, but 'the market ... has eroded the social fibre that gives shape and resilience to the experiences of individuals, families, and ultimately, the market itself'.[3]

This critique of unfettered market processes forms a central tenet of contemporary communitarian political philosophy and social democratic politics. These ideas have a long intellectual history, which includes Marx's depiction of capitalism as a malevolent force that destroyed all pre-existing social institutions,[4] and Ferdinand Tönnies'[5] distinction between the *gemeinschaft* 'community' that predated the market and the more alienating *gesellschaft* 'society' that was created by industrial capitalism.

It is, however, in the writings of Karl Polanyi that contemporary social democrats find their principal inspiration.[6] It was Polanyi who argued that the modern 'market economy' destroys human relationships built on non-market values such as reciprocity and redistribution. According to Polanyi, the 'market economy' did not emerge spontaneously owing to what Adam

2   Newton, K. (1999) 'Social capital and democracy in modern Europe', in van Deth, J., Maraffi, M., Newton, K., Whitely, P. (eds) *Social Capital and European Democracy*, London: Routledge, p. 9.

3   Ciscel, D. H., Heath, J. A. (2001) 'To market, to market: imperial capitalism's destruction of social capital and the family', *Review of Radical Economics*, 33: 401–44, p. 402.

4   Marx, K., Engels, F. (1848/1985) *The Communist Manifesto*, London: Penguin Classics.

5   Tönnies, F. (1887/1955) *Gemeinschaft und Gesellschaft*, trans. C. Loomis, London: Routledge and Kegan Paul.

6   Polanyi, K. (1944) *The Great Transformation*, Boston, MA: Beacon Press.

Smith described as the human propensity to 'truck, barter and exchange', but was the result of imposition by a state heady on the emerging ideology of classical economics. Insofar as markets had existed before this era, these were not based on an impersonal rule of contract and the free play of supply and demand, but were embedded in a network of solidaristic obligations 'administered' by community organisations such as the craftsmen's guilds, and enforced by the state. Seen from this perspective, the widespread movement to regulate markets that occurred towards the end of the nineteenth century and accelerated thereafter with the rise of the welfare state was a 'protective response' to the social destruction wrought by an era when market values were allowed free rein.

Given the miserable performance of state socialism in the twentieth century, contemporary social democratic intellectuals, exemplified by Geoffrey Hodgson and Raymond Plant, are less hostile to the notion of a market economy per se than was Polanyi, but they maintain that market processes should be subordinated by institutions not characterised by contractual exchange. In a sophisticated account, Hodgson echoes Hayek's contention that markets are required to coordinate economic activity under conditions of complexity and dispersed knowledge – conditions that render large-scale central planning unworkable.[7] According to Hodgson, however, while markets are needed to generate price signals reflecting dispersed knowledge about the changing scarcity of different goods, the contractual process that generates such signals depends too heavily on cash incentives. Price-coordinated markets encourage an acquisitive and selfish spirit that

---

7   Hodgson, G. (1998) *Economics and Utopia*, London: Routledge.

undermines trust and respect for contract and property rights. Thus, if it is in the interests of a self-employed lorry driver to fly-tip dangerous waste near a school playground in order to avoid the payment of a disposal fee at a refuse site then markets will do nothing to discourage such behaviour,[8] for 'the cost of moral scruples ... is likely to be business extinction'.[9]

Moral or pro-social behaviour is therefore understood to have many of the properties of a collective good: private individuals will tend to underinvest in it because the benefits that accrue are dispersed throughout society, appear only over a long period of time and are non-excludable (leading to free-rider problems), whereas the costs of moral behaviour are far more personal and immediate. The result, according to Coleman, is that where people rationally choose between self-interest and morality, there is likely to be 'an imbalance in the relative investment in organisations that produce private goods for a market and those associations and relationships in which the benefits are not captured [by those who have created them]'.[10] It is claimed, then, that the introduction of market mechanisms to areas of society traditionally outside their scope leads to the spread of values that undermine the activities and informal associations that generate the social capital upon which the market itself depends.

According to many social democrats this moral free-for-all is further exacerbated by the fact that the value attached to marketed goods is determined purely by the subjective choices of individual consumers and producers. Liberal morals are too 'thin'

8   Page, R. (1996) *Altruism and the British Welfare State*, Aldershot: Ashgate, p. 15.

9   Shaw, P. (1999) 'Markets and moral minimalism', in Norman, R. (ed.) (1999) *Ethics and the Market*, Aldershot: Ashgate, p. 28.

10   Coleman (1988) op. cit., pp. 117–18.

and should be replaced by a view of the individual as a social being whose preferences should be judged against a 'thicker' conception of the common good. Economic liberalism is judged to be 'atomistic' in maintaining that markets allow for the free expression of personal preferences. According to Plant, for example,

> The more the idea takes hold that all goods are to be seen as commodities and thus a matter purely of individual value, the less compelling will be the complementary idea that we need to secure a set of common moral values independent of individual choice. We cannot assume that the extension of the sphere of commodities and individual choice will have no impact at all on general conceptions of morality.[11]

Seen in the above light, markets are parasitic on the social capital needed for their maintenance and will always be unstable in the absence of countervailing institutions governed by different operating norms.

Thus, on Hodgson's view there is a large sphere of relationships that should be immune from the rule of contract. Even 'neoliberals' such as Hayek, he notes, do not believe that relationships within families and between friends should be based on market exchange. Such relations are characterised by altruism or reciprocity, and it is the existence of such non-contractual relationships which sustains social capital. For Hodgson, this creates a contradiction in classical liberal thought. Thus:

> The proponents of market individualism cannot have it both ways. To be consistent with their own arguments, all arrangements must be subject to property, markets and trade. They cannot in one breath argue that the market is the best way of ordering all socio-economic activities, and

11   Plant (1999) op. cit., p. 18.

then deny it in another. If they cherish family values then
they have to recognise the practical and moral limits of
market imperatives and pecuniary exchange.[12]

The family is not, according to this view, the only institution
that provides an important source of non-market norms – the
modern welfare state also represents the institutional embodi-
ment of resource allocation based on reciprocity and buttresses
social capital against the excessive individualism generated by
private markets.

Social democrats such as Hodgson and Plant are not, of
course, unique in making such claims. A related set of arguments
has been made in the 'right-wing' variant of communitarian
theory. Writing from a conservative communitarian perspective,
for example, John Gray contends that market liberalisation and
increasing female labour market participation are contributing to
the destruction of the family and to an increase in crime. Similarly,
according to Gray, contemporary globalisation and the liberalisation of international trade are contributing to the destruction of
the social capital characteristic of non-Western forms of capitalism, such as the 'East Asian' model, and their replacement by
a monolithic form of Anglo-American individualism. Restrictions
on trade and capital flows should, therefore, be implemented in
an attempt to preserve social capital from the destructive effects
of market forces.[13]

For communitarians of 'the right', the freeing of markets in
recent years has also undermined the religious basis of society that
was traditionally an important source of common life and shared

---

12 Hodgson (1998) op. cit., p. 84.
13 Gray, J. (1998) *False Dawn: The Delusions of Global Capitalism*, London: Granta.

values. Exposure to markets is said to weaken religious sources of moral authority by reducing spiritualism to little more than a life-style choice between the competing 'brands' of, say, Catholicism and astrology, or Buddhism and Islam. Thus, according to the Chief Rabbi of the UK, the market is 'a highly anti-traditional force ... [that] encourages a view of human life as a series of consumer choices rather than as a set of inherited ways of doing things', and, 'In the process, religion itself is transformed from salvation to a branch of the leisure industry.'[14]

The decline of traditional social institutions and the common life and shared values that they supported is said then to leave a society in which most relationships are pursued only as a matter of economic expediency. For writers such as Hodgson, Plant and Gray, these relationships are too shallow to form the basis of a healthy civil society, leading to a vicious circle of ever-declining social capital that ultimately threatens the stability of the market order itself.

---

14   Sacks, J. (1999) *Morals and Markets*, London: Institute of Economic Affairs, pp. 12–13.

4 CLASSICAL LIBERALISM, MARKETS AND THE SPONTANEOUS GENERATION OF BRIDGING SOCIAL CAPITAL

The critique of liberal markets sketched in the previous chapter draws heavily on the notion that commercial morals are excessively 'thin'. While writers such as Hodgson, Plant and Gray recognise that markets are necessary to cope with conditions of economic complexity, they maintain that market processes need to be 'kept in their place' in order to sustain the wider social framework of which they are part.

Classical liberalism, markets and the importance of weak ties

If the communitarians are right about the negative relationship between commerce and social capital then some very serious problems arise. The logic of the communitarian position suggests that if we extend the role of markets we reduce levels of trust but, as the more sophisticated communitarians such as Hodgson recognise, if we reduce the role of markets we also reduce the capacity to coordinate social relationships under conditions of complexity. From a classical liberal perspective, however, communitarians are misguided about the relationships necessary to sustain the social fabric. Most critiques of markets and of liberalism more generally focus on a relative decline in *bonding* social capital. Concerns about the decline in religion, traditional values and community solidarity fall clearly into this category. Yet from a classical liberal perspective, it is precisely this type of social capital which should be 'kept in its place' in order to allow looser and more complex bridging relationships to form between people who *differ* in their goals and values.

Communitarian critics tend to hark back to a lost golden age of supposedly higher social trust. To put it mildly, however, it is hard to share the nostalgia for pre-industrial society evident in the work of Marx, Tönnies and Polanyi, for the sort of trust that existed in pre-capitalist societies was far from the generalised social trust necessary to form bridging relationships between largely different people. Solidarism in pre-market society was almost exclusively an *intra*-group phenomenon with inter-group relations characterised by habitual conflict.

As Hayek has argued, it was learning to submit to an impersonal ethos that *did not* require widespread agreement on substantive ends which allowed inter-group relations to become more productive. As links between people increasingly centred on trade, the communitarian ethos of the tribe became confined to small groups such as family, friends and voluntary associations based on face-to-face relations and a common set of ends. Such groupings were, however, embedded in a much wider 'catallactic' order, not governed by any one set of ends, but held together via a nexus of impersonal relations such as contract and respect for property.[1]

Far from being an era of cooperative relationships, it would be better to characterise the pre-industrial era as one ridden with highly exclusive social practices. The guilds, churches and corporatist structures enforced by the pre-industrial state that

---

1   Hayek, F. A. (1988) *The Fatal Conceit*, London: Routledge.

are eulogised in the writings of Karl Polanyi constituted a form of bonding social capital premised on the exclusion of those sections of the population deemed not to conform to prevailing community norms. As Sheilagh Ogilvie has documented in her detailed analyses of guilds and social capital in pre-industrial Germany, not only did the existence of such solidaristic associations and their restrictive practices stifle innovation and economic growth, they also contributed to the systematic exclusion of women, members of ethnic and religious minorities and other 'outcast' groups. In contrast, the more liberal economies of the Netherlands and England, where the state did not enforce the privileges of the guilds, while not without their own forms of exclusion, were much more successful in the promotion of innovation and growth, and provided superior employment opportunities for women and 'unconventionals'.[2]

The development of generalised trust or bridging social capital between actors who are very different from one another necessarily requires that the moral framework shared by these actors is relatively 'thin'. Where people differ in religion, cultural values and other aspects of identity, it is highly unlikely that they will agree on a common set of purposes. In such circumstances attempts to use the power of the state to enforce a shared set of goals are likely to produce conflict as groups compete to capture the governmental apparatus to impose their own particular vision of the good society.[3] The more we rely on shared moral ends as the

2   See, for example, Ogilvie, S. (2003) *A Bitter Living: Women, Markets and Social Capital in Early Modern Germany*, Oxford: Oxford University Press; Ogilvie, S. (2004) 'Guilds, efficiency and social capital: evidence from German proto-industry', *Economic History Review*, 58(2): 286–333.

3   See, for example, Kukathas, C. (2003) *The Liberal Archipelago: A Theory of Diversity and Freedom*, Oxford: Oxford University Press.

basis of social cooperation, the less willing we will be to cooperate with those who are different in their values. If people deal only with those who share the same moral outlook, or trade only with 'locals' rather than engage in international trade with 'foreigners', then the sphere of cooperative relationships will be reduced. One need only refer to the nationalist rhetoric used by protectionist interests and anti-globalisation activists, not to mention the language of religious fundamentalism in its various forms, to recognise that attempts to develop greater 'solidarity' may be as likely to fracture society as to 'unite' it. The development of bridging social capital, therefore, necessarily involves a thin set of morals, such as tolerance of others, the observance of contracts and respect for private property, which can be shared by actors with otherwise diverse and perhaps even conflicting moral codes.

Within the above context, Vincent Ostrom, writing in a distinctly Tocquevillian vein,[4] distinguishes between a 'self-governed' and a 'state-governed' conception of society. The former refers to an order in which people subscribe to self-generating and largely self-enforcing rules of interaction which enable them to go about their separate purposes.[5] People may be members of many different voluntary groups and organisations in order to pursue shared goals, but they are not defined by their membership in any particular group committed to any *one* purpose. In the state-governed conception of society, by contrast, the rules of social interaction are assumed to be created by and enforced by 'the government' in accordance with a 'social purpose' and funds

---

4   Alexis de Tocqueville, the nineteenth-century author of *Democracy in America*, is widely cited as the founding father of research into civil society and social capital.

5   Ostrom, V. (1997) *The Meaning of Democracy and the Vulnerability of Democracies*, Ann Arbor: University of Michigan Press.

are distributed and regulations issued to direct people's behaviour accordingly. The latter understanding of civil order is, according to Ostrom, incompatible with personal freedom and the independence of individuals and voluntary groups from the state.

Ostrom's analysis of self-government in this regard is similar to the understanding of 'civil association' in a liberal order advanced by Oakeshott and Hayek.[6] For these writers, while facilitating *general* purposes such as communication and cooperation, the rules necessary to sustain a healthy civil society are otherwise *purposeless*. Actors identify with communal conventions that order their behaviour, such as linguistic rules and observance of property rights, but such rules are *not* directed towards a specified goal. In the case of language, for example, the words and phrases in common usage emerge through an evolutionary process involving multiple communicative acts not directed towards the achievement of any particular end. Although some such rules, notably those pertaining to the protection of property rights, may be enforced by the state, rules of this type enable actors to pursue a wide variety of diverse and perhaps conflicting purposes. To speak of a 'social purpose' would require that society operate as an 'enterprise association' or '*taxis*' that defines the ends of its citizens and is appropriate only to a closed society defined by a narrow set of goals. As Oakeshott has noted: 'civil freedom is not tied to a choice to be and remain associated in terms of a common purpose: it is neither more nor less than the absence of such a purpose or choice'.[7]

As well as minimising conflict between those who differ in

---

6   Oakeshott, M. (1990) *On Human Conduct*, Oxford: Clarendon Press; Hayek, F. A. (1982) *Law, Legislation and Liberty*, London: Routledge.

7   Oakeshott (1990), op. cit., p. 158.

cultural values, 'thin' moral rules of this nature are required by commerce because most people involved in exchanges are either completely unknown to each other, or known only in a relatively impersonal setting, such as in the relationship between a buyer and a seller. Where contacts between people are of the 'weak' variety it is not possible to evaluate in detail the 'thicker' moral character of the actors concerned (such as their level of attendance at church or mosque, or their sexual peccadilloes), because the information costs involved are excessively high. In situations of commercial exchange the aspects of a person's character that are most pertinent are relatively minimal or 'thin', including such criteria as their contribution to the profit and loss account or their willingness to observe contracts.

The necessity to develop a 'thinner' moral framework brought about by the rise of commerce was, of course, one of the central themes in the writings of the early classical liberals such as Adam Smith and David Hume. It was apparent that the 'strong ties' of clan and kinship that bound together the members of the close-knit groups that constituted traditional society could not extend throughout the Great Society of a modern, advanced economy. As Hume noted, 'sympathy with persons remote from us is much fainter than with persons near and contiguous'.[8] Smith, meanwhile, described the concentric circles of sympathy that emanated outwards from close family to friends, more distant relatives, acquaintances and finally to strangers. He illustrated this phenomenon with the example of how 'a man of humanity in Europe' would be affected by news of a Chinese earthquake. Such

---

8   Hume, D. (1739–40/1985) *A Treatise of Human Nature*, London: Penguin Classics, p. 653. For a recent discussion of this phenomenon, see, for example, Seabright, P. (2004) *The Company of Strangers*, Princeton, NJ: Princeton University Press.

a man would 'first of all express very strongly his sorrow for the misfortune of that unhappy people', and, no doubt, 'make many melancholy reflections upon the precariousness of human life', but, ultimately:

> The most frivolous disaster which could befall himself would occasion a more real disturbance. If he was to lose his little finger to-morrow, he would not sleep to-night; but, provided he never saw them, he will snore with the most profound security over the ruin of a hundred millions of his brethren.[9]

While the globalisation of the media may mean that such disasters are not as distant today as they were in Smith's time – contemporary people of humanity *do* see the victims of tragedies on their television screens and may as a result contribute to an international appeal – the essential point remains: a personal event, such as an injury, or the loss of a family member or close friend/colleague, is likely to cause far more distress than the news of a disaster on another continent in which many thousands perish. It should be emphasised, of course, that in drawing attention to this phenomenon Smith was not making a moral judgement about the relative value of different lives, but was making an empirical observation about the different levels of sympathy people feel towards those who are well known to them relative to those who are not. It is not that people act immorally in failing to care for complete strangers as much as family and friends. Rather, from Smith's point of view, intense feelings of sympathy, which include love and friendship (or for that matter hate), are necessarily reserved for those of whom we have detailed personal

---

9   Smith, A. (1759/1982a) *The Theory of Moral Sentiments*, Indianapolis, IN: Liberty Fund, pp. 136–7.

knowledge, while feelings towards those of whose character we are largely ignorant are 'thinner' in terms of content and intensity.

It follows from this epistemological or knowledge-based recognition of the limits to 'sympathy' that different levels of morality and expectations about the constituents of appropriate conduct are required in different social contexts. As Otteson has argued, the norms that Smith's 'impartial spectator' would observe in relations between family, friends and colleagues are different from those approved between strangers.[10]

The morals expected in commercial relations, which are often between relative strangers or at best acquaintances, will tend to be more impersonal, focused on principles such as the observance of contracts, and will be more oriented towards the self-interest of the parties involved than for the direct benefit of 'others'. This is, from a Smithian perspective, entirely defensible because 'other-regarding' behaviour is appropriate only when people have sufficient knowledge of the personal history, character and needs of the actors concerned. It is not, therefore, that commerce corrupts our sense of morals as communitarians imply, but that the context of commercial exchange requires a different sort of morality. Smith was not of the view that the commercial ethos would pervade the family or other intimate ties, and clearly believed that if people behaved in their more intimate relationships in the way that

---

10 Otteson, J. (2003) *Adam Smith's Marketplace of Life*, Cambridge: Cambridge University Press. In this work Otteson demonstrates convincingly that the so-called 'Adam Smith Problem', i.e. the alleged contradiction between Smith's focus on the capacity of humans to develop norms of empathy and fellow-feeling in *The Theory of Moral Sentiments* and his focus on the primacy of 'self-interest' in *The Wealth of Nations*, is an illusion. As Otteson shows, Smith was attempting to show that different types of social norms and expectations are appropriate in *different* social contexts.

they do in their commercial relationships they would meet with disapproval.

Markets, reputation and the maintenance of weak ties

The question remains, of course, whether the cash nexus and the observance of contracts provide sufficient resources to sustain the 'weak ties' on which they depend. Smith's answer to the question of how to sustain a commercial society was that virtuous behaviour will arise spontaneously because it is in each individual's self-interest to cooperate with others. Wherever commerce is to be found, 'probity and punctuality always accompany it', so that, 'When the greater part of the people are merchants they always bring probity and punctuality into fashion, and these therefore are the principal virtues of a commercial nation.'[11]

Smith believed that in a commercial society it was in each individual's interest to establish a reputation for trustworthiness and probity. 'Honesty is the best policy' because people are unlikely to enter into contracts with people who possess a reputation for underhand dealing. As a consequence of market competition, even individuals who desire only their own personal advancement are led to behave in what is at least a morally tolerable fashion. The freedom to exit from relationships with those who prove undeserving of trust and to enter into new relationships with those who appear more virtuous drives up the general standard of human conduct in the same way that the forces of competition improve the standard of goods and services. The Smithian invisible hand not only guides people towards prosperity, it also guides

---

11   Smith, A. (1766/1982b) *Lectures on Jurisprudence*, Indianapolis, IN: Liberty Fund, pp. 538–9.

them to observe the basic set of morals that sustain the 'weak ties' and social capital on which a commercial society depends.

While Smith's depiction of commercial society anticipated later work suggesting that cooperation can evolve spontaneously among actors pursuing their own interests in repeated exchanges and games,[12] his portrayal of eighteenth-century commerce, along with others who inspired '*le doux commerce*' thesis,[13] was nonetheless based upon experience of transactions among tradespeople who had at least *some* direct personal knowledge of each other. Smith was less convinced, however, that market exchanges could spontaneously produce trust when they are more anonymous or not repeated: 'Where people seldom deal with one another, we find that they are somewhat disposed to cheat, because they can gain more by a smart trick than they can lose by the injury which it does to their character.'[14]

Such a view questions the ability of markets to regulate themselves when exchanges are not repeated, and this view is now reflected in the analysis of information asymmetries[15] put forward by contemporary economists who have sought to resurrect the significance of 'market failure'.[16] According to this perspective,

---

12   For example, Allison, P. (1992) 'The cultural evolution of beneficent norms', *Social Forces*, 71(2): 279–301; Axelrod, R. (1990) *The Evolution of Cooperation*, London: Penguin.

13   The phrase coined by Montesquieu – Montesquieu, Charles-Louis de Secondat, Marquis de (1748/1961) *L'Esprit des Lois*, Paris: Garnier. For a recent and comprehensive statement of the '*doux commerce*' thesis, see McCloskey, D. (2006) *The Bourgeois Virtues: Ethics for a Commercial Age*, Chicago, IL: Chicago University Press.

14   Smith, A. (1766/1982b) op. cit., pp. 538–9.

15   The classic paper in this regard is Akerlof, G. (1970) 'The market for lemons: quality, uncertainty and the market mechanism', *Quarterly Journal of Economics*, 97(4): 543–69.

16   For example, Stiglitz, J. (1994) *Whither Socialism?*, MIT Press.

when consumers lack the information to evaluate the quality of the product being supplied, or the reputation of the supplier, then far from improving average standards competition leads to a decline in the quality of the goods on sale. In a market where, owing to consumer ignorance, there is no reward for trustworthy conduct, unscrupulous suppliers drive out the good, unless the state steps in to perform the quality control function.

As Hayek always emphasised, however, market institutions should be seen as 'discovery processes' which evolve dynamically in ways that even the most far-sighted economist cannot anticipate.[17] Market failure theory predicts that in markets where there are information asymmetries, massive inefficiencies will persist and potentially profitable trades will fail to occur owing to the absence of information and/or trust. What market failure theory has failed to anticipate, however, is the manner in which entrepreneurs have innovated to fill the 'trust gap' and to remove these impediments to trade. Gains from trade have been exploited by entrepreneurs who specialise in checking the trustworthiness of others and who *create* social capital by developing a reputation for supplying appropriate levels of assurance. In doing so, entrepreneurial innovation such as the development of brand names and simple reputation-building devices such as the offer of 'money-back' guarantees has transformed potentially non-repeated exchange scenarios into examples of repeated or iterated transactions. Thus, empirical analyses of markets hypothesised to exhibit asymmetric information, such as those for used automobiles, offer

---

17   Hayek, F. A. (1948) 'The meaning of competition', in Hayek, F. A. (1948) *Individualism and Economic Order*, Chicago, IL: Chicago University Press; Hayek, F. A. (1978) 'Competition as a discovery process', in Hayek, F. A. (1978) *New Studies in Politics, Economics and the History of Ideas*, London: Routledge.

no support for the theoretical claim that competition leads to declining product standards.[18]

Brand-named goods and franchised stores in particular provide an assurance function by reducing information costs and provide an entrepreneurial bridge between otherwise anonymous buyers and sellers. A producer of pharmaceutical goods may, for example, have no contact with the final purchasers of their product, but may have repeat dealings and a relationship of trust with a branded pharmacy outlet, which in turn may have repeat dealings and a reputation for excellence with the final consumers of the good concerned. Markets, therefore, draw on a 'division of trust' in much the same way that Hayek sees the price system drawing on a 'division of knowledge'. What matters is that each link in the chain has an incentive to specialise in developing a reputation for good conduct or to acquire information about the trustworthiness of the particular link that is most relevant to them. In this way, markets economise on the need for trust in much the same way that they economise on the need for other types of knowledge. Just as market participants need know nothing about the majority

---

18   It is remarkable how frequently the 'lemons' model, backed by casual empiricism – 'why is it next to impossible to buy a good used car' – is cited as conclusive proof of 'market failure' resulting from asymmetric information. See, for example, the recent popular text by Harford, T. (2006) *The Undercover Economist*, London: Little, Brown (ch. 5), for an example of this tendency. Authors such as Stiglitz who have done most to advance theories of asymmetric information have not completed *any* empirical work to test the practical relevance of such models. Far from supporting 'market failure' arguments, empirical work that has been conducted in this area demonstrates that it is, in fact, relatively easy 'to find a good used car'. For example, Bond, E. W. (1984) 'A direct test of the "lemons" model: the market for used pick-up trucks', *American Economic Review*, 72(4): 801–804. See also the collection of papers in Cowen, T., Crampton, E. (eds) (2002) *Market Failure or Success: The New Debate*, Cheltenham: Edward Elgar.

of prices in the economy in order to engage in 'economising behaviour'– all they need know about are changes in the price of the final goods that *they* buy[19] – so there is no need for most people to know anything about the trustworthiness or otherwise of the vast majority of market participants; all they need know is the reputation of the particular brands on which they rely. Since most people are, however, involved in overlapping reputational networks, the average level of trustworthiness expected from a person picked out at random in a developed market economy will be quite high. The general pressure to maintain one's reputation exerted in a competitive environment will tend to encourage the internalisation of cooperative norms which will 'keep people honest' even in those situations where they might benefit from shirking behaviour.

In an international marketplace, brand names are a particularly important means of ensuring that consumers without local knowledge receive a guaranteed quality of service. A person may, for example, stay at a franchise outlet such as a Holiday Inn in any major city of the world and be assured of a certain level of cleanliness before she has had the opportunity to learn about the reputations of local hotels. In this case, the Holiday Inn brand acts as the assurance that a particular form of quality control has been exercised on behalf of the consumer. The very existence of such reputational brands in turn acts to raise the average standards offered by the local suppliers in their attempt to attract custom. Brand names, of course, need not guarantee a minimum or basic standard, but may also act as a badge of excellence. Volvo

---

19   On this, see Hayek, F. A. (1948) 'The use of knowledge in society', in *Individualism and Economic Order*, op. cit. See also Friedman, J. (2006) 'Popper, Weber and Hayek: the epistemology and politics of ignorance', *Critical Review*, 17(1–2): 1–58.

and Saab cars have a reputation for superb safety features and longevity, while Rolls-Royce and Aston Martin are known for high quality in engineering and design.

Retailers and other 'middlemen', then, 'supply' the trust and assurance that is 'demanded' to facilitate successful market transactions. Until consumers are confident that a new good or service will provide what it promises, they are unlikely to purchase it. As Klein has noted, for example, an inventor who creates a new power tool 'has not produced a great *product* until he has created assurance'.[20] Brand names are an effective means of providing this assurance. An inventor may sell her product to a trusted third party such as Black and Decker, whose trademark carries the assurance necessary to successfully market the new invention to a wider market. Black and Decker, therefore, 'is not only a manufacturer, distributor and advertiser, it is also a knower that grants its own seal of approval'.[21] The success of a brand depends upon repeat purchases, which requires consumers to be satisfied with the products that carry the particular name.[22]

There are, of course, many other devices routinely used by market participants to discover information about the reputation of others. Educational and professional qualifications, for example, provide information about participants within labour markets. Consumer groups and organisations provide reports on the reliability and quality of different goods and services and their producers. Financial institutions, such as banks and insurance companies, employ specialised organisations to investigate

---

20   Klein, D. (2001) 'The demand for and the supply of assurance', *Economic Affairs*, 21(1): 4–11, p. 6. See also Klein, D. (2000) *Assurance and Trust in a Great Society*, New York: Foundation for Economic Education.

21   Klein (2001) op. cit., p. 6.

22   Ibid. See also Akerlof (1970) op. cit.

the reliability of potential clients; without a good credit rating it is difficult to obtain insurance or to borrow the money required to purchase a house. Moreover, the financial services provided by credit cards and bank accounts are not limited to the obvious unsecured borrowing and convenient organisation of one's finances: the possession of these items also communicates information to others about the reputation of the holder.[23]

Trust is a highly valuable asset for which there is a 'demand', and for this reason it is 'supplied' rather than undermined by the market. While the vast majority of participants within an advanced market economy do not engage in face-to-face exchanges, a host of institutions have developed spontaneously to provide the trust necessary to sustain commercial exchange on a vast scale. Thus, empirical analyses of 'generalised social trust' find no evidence that the proportion of people who exhibit trust in others declines with exposure to market forces. On the contrary, in a cross-country study of over fifty states, Berggren and Jordahl find a strongly positive correlation between the degree of economic freedom in a society (especially the security of property rights) and levels of generalised trust.[24]

None of the above is meant to imply that markets lead to universally trustworthy conduct. There will always be those who engage in scams and crooked deals. What matters is that markets provide mechanisms that reduce the excesses that flow from human imperfections, and, as will be shown in due course, compare very favourably in doing so with the alternative of centralised government controls.

---

23 Klein (2000, 2001) op. cit.
24 Berggren, N., Jordahl, H. (2006) 'Free to trust: economic freedom and social capital', *Kyklos*, 59(2):141–69.

5 MARKETS AND THE MIX BETWEEN BONDING AND BRIDGING SOCIAL CAPITAL

The analysis thus far has highlighted the mechanisms that enable a market economy to maintain bridging social capital. It is important to recognise, however, that while a classical liberal framework places less reliance on the 'bonding' social capital associated with stronger, more personal ties, it does not eliminate such relationships in favour of a society entirely governed by commerce. On the contrary, market institutions provide an environment in which both bridging *and* bonding social capital can coexist, and where relationships and practices conducive to wider cooperation may be promoted.

Families, voluntary associations and the mix between bonding and bridging social capital

Maintaining an appropriate mix between bonding and bridging social capital is crucial because, as Hayek observed, if an advanced society is to function effectively people must learn to live in what might be termed two 'different worlds'.[1] On the one hand they participate in the 'micro-order' of families and family-like groups based on a high degree of personal intimacy and held together by the pursuit of shared ends linked to that very intimacy. On the

---

1   Hayek (1988) op. cit., p. 18.

other hand, however, in order to acquire the goods and services they need to sustain themselves, families must participate in a 'macro-order' of more distant if not anonymous relationships with countless other actors who do not share their specific ends. There is, as a consequence, a tension between the rules of conduct appropriate in family life and intimate relationships and those required in the wider world of commerce and society.

While the tension between the norms exhibited in families and those required in a commercial context is real, the family[2] may nonetheless be seen as a bridge between the 'micro-order' of the small group and the 'macro-order' of the wider society, for it is as children in the context of the family that people first acquire the skills necessary to maintain relationships with others. Within families these skills pertain to intimate contact, but because families are themselves embedded in multiple external relationships characterised by differing degrees of familiarity, they also provide a school for the skills, such as respect for property and possessions, required to maintain one's reputation in more impersonal contexts. These may range from the still relatively personal interactions in schools and voluntary associations to progressively more distant and anonymous business and trade relationships, such as those in firms, where the expectation is that one may judge and be judged on the more unforgiving criteria of contributions to profit and loss.[3]

Viewed through this Hayekian lens, there is no substance to the claims of Hodgson and other social democratic critics that the logic

2 The use of the term 'family' in this context is not confined to the 'nuclear' family and to formal marriages, but may also include other 'family-like' relationships such as those between same-sex couples and close friendships of other sorts.

3 Horwitz, S. (2005) 'The functions of the family in the Great Society', *Cambridge Journal of Economics*, 29: 669–84.

of market liberalism requires the replacement of family-like bonds with a process based entirely on contractual exchange. Commitment to a liberal market does not privilege the role of commercial relationships per se. From a classical liberal perspective all that matters is that individuals and organisations should have the liberty to enter into and exit from relationships with other individuals and organisations as they judge appropriate. In a complex advanced society different sorts of social practices and institutional arrangements compete with one another and may be appropriate in different situations and for different tasks. Reliance on market signals such as the making of profits and losses generated through commercial exchanges is, for example, appropriate where people need to coordinate with many other agents, who do not share their substantive ends, and where reliable mechanisms are required to reduce free-riding or predatory behaviour when actors are not known to one another personally. Family relations, and other groupings based on a shared vocation such as religion or amateur sport, do not typically involve significant coordination problems, as members are usually involved in the pursuit of shared or very similar goals. Insofar as there are free-rider problems in such situations, these are more readily overcome without recourse to the discipline of profit and loss accounting, owing to the relative ease of processing information about and monitoring actors with whom one is intimately familiar.

As Horwitz has argued, there is no more likelihood that a liberal, competitive environment will lead to the elimination of the family than that it will lead to the elimination of other institutions such as the firm.[4] Unlike families, firms are organisations

---

4   Ibid.

that must mobilise cooperation from larger numbers of people who may *not* share common ends, and may require mechanisms such as performance-related pay to control problems of shirking and free-riding. The internal operations of firms are largely hierarchical and reflect the efficiency advantages that can be gained from replacing the decentralised bargaining of 'spot contracts' and 'piecework' with an internal system of command and control.[5] Organisations such as firms are, however, embedded in a meta-level environment of market competition in which the quality of their governance structures, their reputation for probity and capacity to deliver goods to consumers are tested against those of rivals. Firms, therefore, suppress *internal* competition, but are subject to *external* market forces resulting from the decentralised decisions of hundreds and thousands, if not millions, of consumers and investors. Thus, owner-manager firms, joint-stock companies, worker cooperatives and mutual associations all compete for reputation, sales and investment capital.

If organisations such as firms (and different firm structures) have advantages in certain domains, then so too do families. Among the most obvious of these is the provision of conditions conducive to the personal intimacy that most people desire. Families or family-like structures provide an environment in which detailed, personal knowledge of the partners' tastes and values can be developed to the mutual advantage of those concerned. Intimacy of this nature is, of course, particularly relevant in terms of child-raising, where parents or other family members are more likely to have specialised knowledge of their child's proclivities than even the most highly qualified educational experts.

---

5   Coase, R. H. (1937) 'The nature of the firm', *Economica*, 4: 386–405.

Families may, of course, 'contract out' certain functions to individuals and firms in the wider market rather than perform them 'in house'. Which goods and services are purchased commercially rather than produced in the household will vary depending on the preferences and opportunity costs of the families concerned. High-income households, for example, may spend proportionately more time working and may purchase childcare, dry-cleaning and eating-out rather than perform these tasks themselves. As Horwitz points out, however, these dynamics do not necessarily imply a decline in intimacy and bonding. In the case of childcare, for example, parents are still in the best position to tailor their choice of provider to the character of their child. Similarly, as the 'economic' functions of the family such as cleaning and food preparation shift to the market, the time saved on these tasks may enable the family to pursue additional 'non-economic' activities with their children, such as participation in sports or leisure.[6]

Just as the boundaries between firms and the wider market are fluid, shifting with developments in technology and changes in individual preferences, so too are the boundaries between families, voluntary associations and the market. This fluidity does not, however, imply that commercial relationships are ever likely to replace the close-knit bonds that people want to form in families, with friends and to a lesser extent as members of intermediary organisations such as sports clubs. Neither does it imply that the state has the knowledge or capacity to determine the appropriate position of the relevant boundaries, any more than it is able to decide effectively which elements of a firm's production should be 'contracted out' or provided 'in house'. Hodgson's claim that

6   Horwitz (2005) op. cit.

'neo-liberals' contradict their argument about the general superiority of markets by not advocating their extension into families is, therefore, puzzling. It is surely Hodgson's error to suggest that the modern welfare state embodies the norms of altruism and reciprocity found in family-like groups, which he claims need the protection of the state from markets. The delivery of health and education by large impersonal bureaucracies hardly meets the level of intimacy found in families. As we will see in Chapter 8, it is precisely in these more impersonal circumstances that problems associated with predatory rent-seeking behaviour are likely to emerge because competition is *not* permitted to develop.

To be fair, what Hodgson may have in mind here is an argument originally made by Kenneth Arrow.[7] According to Arrow, in areas such as healthcare and education, where asymmetric information may lead to potential market failures, codes of conduct and norms of public service may be inculcated by professional bodies whose members adhere to rules that enjoin them *not* to exploit their superior information. This is a pertinent example of how different organisational structures may be appropriate in different contexts of social interaction. It is, however, difficult to sustain the claim that such professional norms can *only* arise within the confines of a monopolistic welfare state – the Hippocratic Oath did, after all, predate the creation of the UK's National Health Service. Professional associations and standards-setting bodies can and do operate in markets, performing equivalent functions to franchise chains and brand-name capital in other sectors with competition for reputation between different codes of practice. Many organisations with different internal cultures

---

7   Arrow, K. (1963) 'Uncertainty and the welfare economics of medical care', *American Economic Review*, 53(5): 941–73.

can coexist in markets: not-for-profits, cooperatives, mutual associations and partnerships such as John Lewis, for example, attempt to develop an internal ethos and service culture that differ from those in owner-managed firms and joint-stock companies. As we will see below, even the latter frequently attempt to inculcate values such as team spirit in the workforce as part of a wider competitive strategy.

Far from preserving such institutional and motivational diversity, government regulation often acts to discourage it. Ricketts, for example, has shown how regulation of the financial services industry may have accelerated the trend away from mutual ownership of building societies.[8] With detailed government regulation of lending practices now conducted by bodies such as the Financial Services Authority, financial institutions no longer have much reason to compete on grounds of reputation and ethos. Previously, while rates of return may have been less than with conventional banks, consumers often opted for building societies and mutuals on grounds of lower risk and a preference for the values embedded in their particular governance structure. With the governance of financial institutions now regulated by the FSA, however, there is no longer a reason to favour a mutual or not-for-profit bank over more conventional investor-owned enterprises. The removal of the capacity to compete on the reputation and ethos of the governance structure has led building societies to become conventional commercial banks which tend to compete on price alone.

The theoretical weaknesses of the social democratic critique are mirrored by the empirical evidence concerning the effect of liberal markets on cultural and associational life. There is, for

---

8   Ricketts, M. (2000) 'Competitive processes and the evolution of governance structures', *Journal des Economistes et des Etudes Humaines*, 10(2/3): 235–52.

example, little evidence to suggest that when monetary payment for sex is legalised a higher proportion of people consider prostitution a desirable form of sexual relationship.[9] Even a cursory glance at the contemporary political economy and culture of the USA offers scant support for the claim that more market-oriented societies are characterised by conformity to pecuniary relations. The USA continues to exhibit very high rates of volunteer service compared with European countries,[10] has one of the highest rates of religious observance in the developed world, and exhibits the highest rate of private (as opposed to governmental) aid to developing countries.[11] Taking into account also the coexistence of traditional groupings such as the Amish with a modern market economy, a thorough examination of the cultural landscape of the USA is hardly suggestive of the motivational conformity that social democratic critics of US capitalism frequently portray.

Empirical evidence also casts doubt on Putnam's so-called 'bowling alone' thesis: the view that with more people in contemporary market economies spending time on 'private' pursuits such as watching television, they are increasingly less likely to be involved in the voluntary organisations that sustain social capital. According to Putnam, rather than joining organised bowling clubs and leagues as in the past, contemporary Americans are more likely to participate in one-off, private bowling games in

---

9   Epstein, R. (2003) *Skepticism and Freedom*, Chicago, IL: Chicago University Press, pp. 147–8.

10   See, for example, Beito, D. (2000) *From Mutual Aid to the Welfare State*, Chapel Hill: University of North Carolina Press; Skocpol, T. (1996) 'Unravelling from above', *American Prospect*, 25: 20–25.

11   According to findings by the Hudson Institute, US private giving abroad comes close to the *total* amount of official government aid from all donor countries combined – see the Global Index on Philanthropy, New York: Hudson Institute.

closed, intimate groups.[12] Putnam supports these conclusions with longitudinal evidence from the USA showing a decline in the membership of bowling leagues and other such clubs. While it may be true that membership of some associations has declined owing to technological and behavioural changes, Putnam's thesis fails to give sufficient weight to the manner in which the same changes have created new forms of social contact. Membership of bowling leagues in the USA may well have declined, but other groupings not accounted for in his sample such as soccer/football leagues have witnessed enormous growth and on some estimates have increased at a faster rate than population growth.[13] In the UK context, meanwhile, Hall's analysis also suggests a similar lack of empirical support for the supposed decline in associational life.[14]

The decidedly mixed nature of the findings on the trajectory of social capital is not surprising. Longitudinal studies of voluntary groups are subject to a variant of the deficiencies associated with central economic planning: in a dynamic social context it is impossible for any one social scientist or group of social scientists to anticipate the evolution of civil society. Many newly emerging groups fail to appear on a particular analyst's 'radar screen', and it is difficult to see how new forms of social contact, such as the enormous growth in online forums,[15] could ever be properly accounted for in such analyses. This is not to deny the possibility

12   Putnam, R. D. (2000) *Bowling Alone*, New York: Simon and Schuster.

13   Ladd, E. (1996) 'The data just don't show a decline in America's social capital', *Public Prospect*, 7(4): 7–16. See also Schudson, M. (1995) 'What if civic life didn't die?', in Verba, S., Scholzman, K., Brady, H. (1995) *Voice and Equality: Civic Voluntarism in American Politics*, Cambridge, MA: Harvard University Press.

14   Hall, P.A. (1999) 'Social capital in Britain', *British Journal of Political Science*, 29: 417–61.

15   For a discussion of the Internet as a new form of social capital, see Hardin, R. (2004) *Trust*, Cambridge: Polity Press, ch. 5.

that associational ties may decline owing to technological and economic change. On balance, however, both technology-induced and market-induced change seem likely to be neutral in terms of their overall effect on civil society. While such changes may erode certain forms of social capital, they seem just as likely to generate new and unexpected forms of associational life.

Firms and the mix between bonding and bridging social capital

The market economy, then, constitutes a 'macro' environment which sustains a variety of non-commercial bonds at the 'micro' level, such as those found in families and voluntary groups. Even commercial relationships, however, also create opportunities to generate bonding social capital of their own. If social capital is composed of relations that are reproduced or transformed through social interaction then it can also be produced by people who interact with one another in markets. People may, for example, develop friendships in the workplace or at business conferences and may even meet romantic partners at the supermarket checkout. More importantly, the 'weak' interactions that characterise commercial relationships bring together people from many different social and cultural backgrounds and in so doing may create opportunities for the development of new social bonds and shifting identities. It is precisely because people enter markets in order to pursue commercial gain that they tend, at the margin, to be less concerned with the religious or ethnic origin of the partners with whom they exchange and, as a consequence, expose themselves to the unfamiliar through market transactions. The development of bridging social capital in this manner may in turn facilitate new forms of bonding social capital as people are alerted to alternative lifestyles and identities through the everyday inter-actions involved in commercial life. Such processes may include development of cross-cultural friendships and even deeper bonds, such as office romances and marriages between people from different cultures who might never have met were it not for their participation in the 'impersonal' world of work and commer-cial exchange.[16] It is partly for this reason that Hayek frequently used the Greek term 'catallaxy' to describe the market economy, the original meaning of which was to 'change from enemy into a friend'.[17]

In addition, market relationships are often composed of indi-viduals *working together within firms* who, as von Mises put it, 'coop-erate in competition and compete in cooperation'.[18] The relative capacity of firms to develop an internal culture conducive to such dynamics as 'team spirit' and loyalty is a key factor in their ability to deliver products in a competitive way. Consider in this context the spread of Japanese working practices to the USA in the 1980s. Prior to this period, American auto firms had for many years been organised in a hierarchical or 'Taylorist' manner with a strict line of command between senior managers, middle managers and shop floor workers. By the 1980s, however, Taylorist organisa-tions were lagging in productivity and losing money relative to Japanese plants that operated flatter management structures. The latter practices promoted greater levels of trust between

---

16 Storr, V. (2008) 'The market as a social space: on the meaningful extra-economic conversations that can occur in markets', forthcoming in *Review of Austrian Eco-nomics*.

17 See Hayek, F. A. (1982) *Law, Legislation and Liberty*, London: Routledge, Volume 2, p. 108.

18 Mises, L. von (1949) *Human Action*, Yale University Press, p. 345.

workers and management owing to the culture of responsibility engendered on the shop floor and thereby reduced the transaction costs of production. Owing to their greater profitability, Japanese working practices were increasingly imitated by American firms. In this case, open competition and the account of profit and loss stimulated not only significant product improvements but also the spread of management cultures more conducive to workplace cooperation.[19] Had the protectionist policies now advocated by critics of free trade such as Gray been put in place, it is doubtful that such cultural learning and the spread of new forms of social capital would have proceeded as quickly if at all.

Not only do most individuals work together within firms, but many firms enjoy cooperative as well as competitive relationships; most have long-standing arrangements with other firms which supply the factors of production and services necessary for their own successful operation. As Lorenz has noted, relations between firms and their subcontractors are often akin to a partnership based upon mutual dependency, cooperation and trust, where short-term gain will often be sacrificed for the benefits of long-term collaboration.[20]

While it is true that people are unlikely to work in the same firms or even the same industries for their entire working lives, giving greater opportunity to learn more varied skills and to meet with different people, it is not the case that firms will hire and fire employees on the basis of the slightest economic fluctuation. On the contrary, one of the fundamental economic phenomena

19 On this see Fukuyama, F. (2001) *The Great Disruption*, London: Profile Books.

20 Lorenz, E. (1988) 'Neither friends nor strangers: informal networks of subcontracting in French industry', in Gambetta, D. (ed.) (1988) *Trust: Making and Breaking Cooperative Relations*, Oxford: Basil Blackwell.

explored by neoclassical economics has been the labour market rigidities caused by wage 'stickiness' – the fact that wages do not respond to supply and demand conditions as flexibly as they might because (among other reasons) employers may be reluctant to lower the wages of existing employees or employ new workers willing to work for lower salaries out of loyalty to their existing staff.[21] A successful business enterprise needs to strike a delicate balance between the dangers of excessively friendly bonds between workers and managers on the one hand, and the loss of loyalty resulting from excessively distant and impersonal processes on the other.

Culture, ethnicity and the mix between bonding and bridging social capital

If the competitive position of firms is a function of the ability to strike a balance between bonding and bridging social capital, so in a market environment different social norms prove themselves more or less compatible with the wider social networks necessary for economic success. The experience of different ethnic and immigrant groups is particularly instructive in this regard. Many such groups often find it difficult to access credit and employment opportunities on arrival in a new society because they do not possess the reputational signals, such as credit ratings or a bank

---

21 Evidence of wage 'stickiness' in this context does not constitute 'market failure'. It simply confirms that market forces do not behave in the mechanistic manner set out in neoclassical models. There is little or no reason to believe that government action could arrive at a more efficient set of wage rates given the inability of planners to access highly dispersed information concerning supply and demand conditions in the labour market and their complex interaction with the cultural norms of workers and employers.

account, that are taken for granted by established members of the society concerned. In this context, the most successful immigrant communities have been those that have mobilised their own internal bonds to generate the reputational resources necessary to link with the wider community. Korean immigrants to the USA in the 1970s, for example, were often capital-poor and lacked English language skills. The close-knit nature of the Korean community, however, enabled its members to offer low-cost savings and credit services to one another, which facilitated the rapid development of a merchant class specialised in construction, restaurants and the grocery trade. In this instance, the bonds in the Korean community encouraged the accumulation of capital, which in turn allowed the development of reputational links with the wider society, as evidence of property ownership enabled Korean entrepreneurs to obtain bank accounts and credit from formal financial institutions.[22]

Membership of particular ethnic or religious groupings can also offer other advantages in developing linkages with a broader range of social actors, especially in the context of commercial exchange. Chamlee-Wright, for example, notes the reputation for fair dealing that was associated with Quaker merchants in the eighteenth and nineteenth centuries. In such cases the distinctive manner, dress or speech, maintained internally out of commitment to a religious faith or other cultural norms, may also carry economic benefits by providing the right set of reputational

---

22   Chamlee Wright, E. (2006) 'Fostering sustainable complexity in the microfinance industry', *Conversations on Philanthropy*, 3: 23–49. See also Landa, J. (1995) *Trust, Ethnicity and Identity: Beyond the New Institutional Economics of Ethnic Trading Networks, Contract Law and Gift-Exchange*, Ann Arbor: University of Michigan Press; Sowell, T. (1996) *Migrations and Cultures: A World View*, New York: Basic Books.

signals to those outside the group.[23] Seen in this context cultural 'stereotypes' often perform an equivalent function to reputational brands in the marketplace, and in those parts of the developing world where global and even national brands are often absent may be the primary mechanism that actors use when judging whether or not to enter a particular exchange. In conditions of bounded rationality, where actors lack full information, people frequently rely on habits and rules of thumb based on cultural symbolism as a way of reducing the cost of searching for the most trustworthy agents.

Within this context it must be recognised that not all bonding social capital is conducive to successful external linkages. Just as there are differences in the quality of the social and behavioural skills transmitted by families in terms of their capacity to link with the macro-social order, so too there are differences between the compatibility of various cultural norms and the behaviour necessary to promote economic development.

The persistence of poverty across several generations among some immigrant groups, compared with the simultaneous rise of others, suggests that not all forms of bonding social capital are well adapted in this regard. While the persistence of immigrant poverty in some contexts may be the product of outright racism in the surrounding society, the rise out of poverty of other groups that have experienced similar racism suggests that this is not always the dominant factor at play.[24] Consider, for example, the

---

23   Chamlee-Wright (2006) op. cit.

24   According to figures published by the UK Department for Education and Skills and a recent report by the Rowntree Foundation there are substantial differences in educational achievement between working-class male children (defined as those who are in receipt of free school meals) across various ethnic and cultural groups – with the 'White British' category exhibiting the worst performance with

experience of the tens of thousands of Asian traders expelled from Uganda by Idi Amin in 1972, who, with only the possessions they could carry, went on to prosper in every country to which they migrated. Similarly, the repeated commercial success of ethnic and religious groups such as the Chinese, Jews, Gujarati Indians, the Ibos of Nigeria and the Lebanese in a variety of different countries would appear to imply that some types of bonding social capital exhibit a competitive advantage relative to others.[25] A competitive market, therefore, while not hostile to bonding social capital per se, may well exhibit selective pressure in favour of those 'cultural brands' that enable the formation of wider social linkages.

Recognising the tendency for a competitive market to select in favour of certain cultural norms does not, however, imply movement towards the Anglo-American monoculture that critics of globalisation frequently portray. A global marketplace offers competitive niches to a wide variety of ethno-cultural types, each of which may exercise a comparative advantage in particular economic domains. Certain cultural norms, such as those emphasising team spirit, may, for example, prevail in sectors requiring large-scale capital outlays and joint production (such as automobile manufacture), while in other industries a competitive advantage may be exercised by a culture that allows greater room for individual flair (such as textiles and fashion). Historically,

---

a mere 17 per cent achieving five or more GCSE grades A*– C. The comparable figure for the Chinese category is close to 70 per cent, for the Indian over 40 per cent, Bangladeshi 38 per cent, Pakistani 32 per cent, Black African 30 per cent and Black Caribbean 19 per cent. Differences of this order *within* the lower-income category are probably best explained by differences in the cultural emphasis placed on educational achievement between the different groups – see Rowntree (2007) *Tackling Educational Underachievement*, York: Rowntree Foundation.

25   Sowell (1996) op. cit.

Japanese culture has thrived in the former context, whereas the sole-proprietor model of entrepreneurship associated with the Chinese has performed better in the latter.[26] Max Weber famously argued that Protestant culture inspired the work ethic necessary for economic growth in the West, but as Deepak Lal has argued, the strong Confucian values present in East Asian culture now appear to exhibit a competitive advantage relative to a Western model that has witnessed an erosion of such asceticism.[27]

As Caplan and Cowen note, when discussing the effects of international markets on cultural diversity, it is crucial to recognise the difference between diversity as a 'menu of choice' and diversity as 'cultural distinctiveness'.[28] In terms of consumption patterns, markets and trade tend to increase the former, while reducing the latter. Thus, trade between France and the UK means that French products, such as fine cheeses, which were previously available only in France, are now consumed by the British, and British popular music is now widely consumed in France. In this case both France and the UK become *internally* more diverse, with a greater range of choices for their citizens, but the differences *between* the respective countries become less marked as a direct consequence of trade.

On the production side, however, increasing returns to specialisation may operate to intensify regional distinctiveness. As the size of the international market expands, different regions of the world can increase their income by specialising in particular

---

26 Lavoie, D., Chamlee-Wright, E. (2001) *Culture and Enterprise*, London: Routledge.

27 Lal, D. (2001) *Unintended Consequences: The Impact of Factor Endowments, Culture and Politics on Long-Run Economic Performance*, Cambridge, MA: MIT Press.

28 Caplan, B., Cowen, T. (2004) 'Do we underestimate the benefits of cultural competition?', *American Economic Review*, 94(2): 402–407.

production lines – thus Hollywood produces more movies, but Paris and Milan are capitals of couture. These specialisations may in turn act to reinforce the cultural distinctiveness of the particular regions and communities concerned. In a competitive market, it should be emphasised, even cultural practices that exhibit no absolute advantage in their contribution to production or entre-preneurial ingenuity are unlikely to be eradicated entirely owing to the law of comparative advantage. In the context of global trade the international product can be enlarged if different cultural types specialise in those lines where they have the lowest oppor-tunity cost of production. Even the most inefficient producers/cultures have a *comparative* advantage in some markets, though they may lack any *absolute* advantages. Logically, it follows that *all* cultural types possess a comparative advantage in at least some lines of production, even if they have an absolute advantage in none.[29]

---

29 For more on the concept of 'cultural comparative advantage', see Lavoie and Chamlee-Wright (2001) op. cit., ch. 4.

6 SOCIAL CAPITAL, SOCIAL DEMOCRACY AND THE CASE FOR THE ENABLING STATE

Readers of the argument thus far may concede that a classical liberal framework of open markets and limited government is not antithetical to the maintenance of social capital. Even if these arguments are accepted, however, it may still be contended that positive state action is required to promote such capital owing to the wider benefits to other institutions, such as the smooth functioning of the democratic process, that it provides. This line of argument constitutes a second set of social democratic claims: namely, that governments acting in the manner of an 'enabling' state can and should adopt policies that help to 'build' social capital and bridging social capital in particular.

Social capital and democracy

One of the most important claims made for social capital in 'third way' arguments is that it has the power to 'make democracy work'. At the most basic level, it is argued that social capital ensures high levels of voter turnout and popular participation in other aspects of democratic politics, such as membership of political parties. It is suggested, therefore, that many of the problems facing contemporary democracies, such as low voter turnout, distrust of politicians and disillusionment with established political parties, may be ameliorated if the stock of social capital can be increased by state action.[1]

Social capital and the provision of collective goods

At a deeper level, bridging social capital is said to 'make democracy work' by facilitating collective action in the political realm. Not only does it encourage people to vote and to join political parties, it is also said to encourage people to support 'necessary' government interventions and more 'progressive' policies. According to Warren, for example, generalised social trust enables progressive public policies to be implemented because it overcomes popular fears about the likely outcomes. Where there is little trust in other people, uncertainty about how others will react to political initiatives may reduce people's willingness to vote for or participate in collective action.[2] Seen in this context, support for government provision of those collective goods believed to be undersupplied by the market economy will not be forthcoming in the absence of widespread public trust in political institutions.

Social capital and policy success

High levels of social capital are not only believed to increase the likelihood that public policy interventions will be attempted; it is

1   For example, Brehm, J., Rhan, W. (1997) 'Individual-level evidence for the causes and consequences of social capital', *American Journal of Political Science*, 41: 999–1023; Putnam (1993) op. cit.; Putnam (2000) op. cit.; Uslaner, E. (1999) 'Democracy and social capital', in Warren, M. E. (ed.) *Democracy and Trust*, Cambridge: Cambridge University Press.

2   Warren, M. E. (1999) 'Introduction', in Warren, M. E. (ed.) *Democracy and Trust*, Cambridge: Cambridge University Press.

also argued that the presence of strong social capital increases the likelihood that these interventions will prove successful. Boix and Posner, for example, argue that social capital provides a powerful new variable that can explain and determine government performance.[3] Boix and Posner suggest that social capital can make government intervention more effective by some combination of the following five factors: the willingness of an engaged electorate to select competent representatives and punish incompetent ones; reduced transaction costs of public policy where the public are generally cooperative and supportive of government; higher quality of inputs into the political process from a more informed and reflective citizenry; increased effectiveness of government bureaucracies where cooperation between agencies and people is the norm; and greater willingness of competing elites to cooperate with one another, rather than seeking to undermine alternative policy proposals.

Strategies for building social capital

If a lack of social capital lies behind the malfunctioning of democratic processes then, according to contemporary social democratic theory, positive government action is needed to stimulate its development. In the words of Dowley and Silver, a belief in the democracy-enhancing qualities of social capital may produce public policies informed by the view that 'If democracy needs civil society, we will support civil society, we will fund voluntary organisations, we will make social capital wherever it is lacking'.[4]

---

3   Boix, C., Posner, D. N. (1998) 'Social capital: explaining its origins and effects on government performance', *British Journal of Political Science*, 28(4): 686–93.
4   Dowley, K. M., Silver, B. D. (2002) 'Social capital, ethnicity and support for

Strategies to build social capital usually involve a programme of institutional redesign focused on public service delivery and the provision of financial assistance to voluntary organisations and the representatives of 'civil society'.

Attempts to involve civil associations directly in the design and provision of state services constitute the first strand of 'third way' strategies to build social capital in this regard. The claim here is that 'public participation' in service provision avoids the failures of 'top-down' bureaucratic planning by ensuring that planners receive information from multiple actors or stake-holders who have better access to 'on the ground' knowledge.[5] Improving the flow of information between service providers and civil society is considered central to a strategy based on the building of trust because it removes the sense that public policy is something that is 'done to' the community and creates a dynamic in which voluntary organisations help to craft public policies for themselves. Granting access to the policy machine is also thought conducive to a more transparent and accountable form of decision-making in which special interest demands give way to a more rounded politics where politicians and civil servants earn the trust of service users at large.[6] The development of trust, it is claimed, will itself improve the quality of policy delivery as both citizens and producers cooperate directly with the government rather

democracy in post-communist states', *Europe-Asia Studies*, 54(4): 505. See also Leigh and Putnam (2002) op. cit.; Hooghe and Stolle (2003) op. cit.

5 For example, Brown, L. D., Ashman, D. (1996) 'Participation, social capital and inter-sectoral problem solving: African and Asian cases', *World Development*, 24: 1467–79; Lam, W. F. (1996) 'Institutional design of public agencies and co-production: a study of irrigation systems in Taiwan', *World Development*, 24: 1039–54; Ritchey-Vance, M. (1996) 'Social capital, sustainability and working democracy: new yardsticks for grassroots development', *Grass Roots Development*, 20: 3–9.

6 Healey, P. (1997) *Collaborative Planning*, London: Macmillan.

than seeking to thwart official objectives. Participation, therefore, generates trust, which improves policy delivery, which in turn generates more trust and so on, in a virtuous circle of accumulating social capital.

'Third way' ideas about the need for greater 'participation' have become highly influential in both developed and developing countries and have been proposed as an alternative to the 'pure' models of market provision or top-down state planning. Within this context, terms such as 'co-production' and 'governance not government' have become buzzwords in the social democratic policy lexicon. In the UK, many of the initial moves in this direction were an unintended consequence of the public service reforms advanced by the Thatcher administration. The inability of the Conservative government of the 1980s to push through the outright privatisation of services such as housing, education, health and social care led to a halfway-house scenario in which provision was contracted out to a range of private sector or voluntary/charitable bodies, leading to a network configuration in place of the more hierarchical structure of traditional public sector monopolies. This approach was subsequently adopted as a deliberate strategy by the New Labour administration with the expressed belief that the participation of civil associations in public sector provision could avoid the failures of top-down central planning, without recourse to the individualist approach that was associated with outright privatisation. In the developing world, meanwhile, 'participationist' ideas lie at the core of new interventionist strategies adopted by the World Bank and various branches of the United Nations. Aid monies and debt relief programmes are now frequently contingent on evidence of states having provided opportunities for non-governmental organisations and other 'stakeholders' to contribute to the formulation of development plans.[7]

The second strand of social capital building in social democratic theory involves the supply of public subsidies to voluntary organisations and so-called 'third sector' groups. The provision of financial aid to 'civil society' assumes that many individuals and communities lack the resources to build up voluntary organisations on their own. Poorer communities, it is argued, typically exhibit lower levels of civil association than the middle classes, and this feeds through into lower levels of participation in the political process. Following Putnam, it is suggested that there is a correlation between membership of civil associations and the propensity of people to participate in the democratic process – for example, an individual who attends church or school parent association meetings is more likely to vote or to participate in a local authority consultation exercise. Much of the current UK government's 'New Deal for Communities', in which billions of pounds have been spent in an attempt to create 'strong communities' in poorer neighbourhoods, draws explicitly on this conception of social capital and the related notion of 'capacity-building'.

Building social capital via the funding of non-governmental organisations has been extremely influential in the UK context, but it has been even more pronounced in terms of the policies adopted by both governments and international aid organisations in their approach to the problem of governance in the developing world. It is argued that the failure of democratic institutions in much of the 'Third World' and in some of the 'transition economies' of the

---

7   See, for example, Easterly, W. (2006) *The White Man's Burden: Why the West's Efforts to Aid the Rest Have Done So Much Ill and So Little Good*, Oxford: Oxford University Press.

former Soviet bloc has been caused by the absence of an effective civil society. Seen in this light, the dominance of one-party political systems and/or the legacy of a 'top-down' form of colonial rule has stifled the emergence of non-governmental organisations, which stand between the state and the market. In the absence of these civil groupings it is argued that societies lack the trust necessary to sustain functioning market institutions and similarly lack the democratic or civic culture necessary to keep a check on the potentially predatory actions of the state.

A related argument suggests that the existence of civil associations increases the probability that societies can overcome 'tragedy of the commons' scenarios which are often at the root of resource depletion. Based on both developed and developing countries, Elinor Ostrom's work[8] demonstrates that solutions to the tragedy of the commons (or tragedy of *open access*, as it should really be known)[9] are not exhausted by the polar alternatives of establishing private or state ownership rights over previously non-owned resources. Where local resource users have established relations of trust, they have been able to manage resources sustainably without recourse to formal private property rights or to government regulation. Many examples from both developed and developing nations suggest that communities can find ways of spontaneously managing resources including mountain forests

---

8   For example, Ostrom, E. (1990) *Governing the Commons: The Evolution of Institutions for Collective Action*, Cambridge: Cambridge University Press.

9   As is now widely recognised, 'common property' arrangements are not to be confused with the 'open access' arrangements associated with the 'tragedy of the commons'. The latter refers to a situation where a resource or asset lacks *any* form of organisational structure to manage the asset in question. Common property regimes, by contrast, typically involve control over a resource by an identifiable user group that regulates access on the basis of customary norms.

and meadows, water for irrigation, coastal fisheries and, more recently, recreation and wildlife.

Building on these insights, international development agencies such as the World Bank have argued that in place of traditional government-to-government aid programmes, which led to various 'aid disasters', especially in Africa, where monies were siphoned off by ruling elites, the emphasis of contemporary development strategy should focus on a 'third way' strategy of 'capacity building' and social capital. Although government-to-government aid is still the dominant form of international assistance, from a position where virtually no money was spent on voluntary associations in the late 1970s and early 1980s, by 1995 8.5 per cent of governmental aid to developing countries was devoted to civil society programmes. The United States Agency for International Development (USAID) alone increased spending on civil society programmes by 320 per cent during the period 1991–98, a trend that has continued to the present time.[10]

---

10 Coyne, C. (2006) 'Reconstructing weak and failed states', *Journal of Social, Political and Economic Studies*, 31(2): 143–62.

7 SOCIAL CAPITAL AND THE ENABLING STATE: AN AUSTRIAN PERSPECTIVE

It should now be evident that social democratic arguments for an 'enabling state' and more democratic participation place great store in the belief that policy failures stem not from any inherent weaknesses of government action, but from a lack of sufficient trust in political institutions. This is a surprising analysis, for if democratic governments have failed to generate the necessary trust in the past, then it is far from clear why they will do so in the future. One might even argue that declines in trust towards political institutions recorded throughout the majority of liberal democracies reflect the fact that people previously displayed *too much* trust in elected governments to address problems that were simply not in their power to solve.

There is, therefore, a strange circularity to the arguments advanced in favour of using more participatory democracy to build social capital. On the one hand it is claimed that social capital is needed to 'make democracy work', yet the strategies proposed in order to build social capital require more democratic participation. From the perspective of both the Austrian and the public choice schools of political economy, however, there are in fact strong theoretical reasons to doubt that it is lack of trust which prevents effective public participation in policymaking. These classical liberal insights suggest that the pathologies of state planning apply not only to orthodox models of government action, but in equal measure to the new and more fashionable raft of interventions intended to cultivate social capital. This chapter sets out an Austrian critique of the enabling state, while Chapter 8 turns to the implications of public choice theory.

Markets and the Austrian critique of democratic planning

Inspired by the legacy of Hayek and von Mises, an Austrian perspective points to fundamental epistemological problems *inherent* in state-centric forms of decision-making. Seen in this light, relative to a market economy based on dispersed though unequal ownership of property, a system of state planning, even when subject to 'public participation', is unable to respond as quickly and effectively to dispersed information about constantly changing socio-economic conditions.

An advanced market economy generates and processes vastly more knowledge than the systems that are at the centre of political decision-making because the former draws widely on the discrete choices of multiple individuals and organisations informed by dispersed knowledge of cultural values (including knowledge of personal or organisational trustworthiness), personal preferences, the availability of substitutes and entrepreneurial innovations. This dispersed knowledge is known only to the individuals and organisations themselves. Crucially, the capacity to coordinate these dispersed 'bits' of information does not exist in any one centre of control, but is transmitted across the overlapping perspectives of dispersed social actors via the price system. Every decision to buy or not to buy, to sell or not to sell, to follow one career or another, contributes incrementally to the formation of prices, transmitting a small piece of information in coded form to those with whom one exchanges. The latter may then adapt their behaviour (substituting more for less expensive alternatives, for example) in light of their own priorities and knowledge, which informs subsequent transactions with still other agents, in a network of ever increasing complexity. What matters is that in order to coordinate their behaviour by economising in response to shifts in the relative scarcity of different goods, actors need not know very much about the complex chain of events that contributes to a rise or fall in price – what they do need to know is that the prices they face have changed.[1]

From an Austrian perspective, compared with markets, democratic participation is a slow and cumbersome mechanism for adjusting to dynamic social conditions. Electing politicians and planners does not improve their capacity to gather and process information that is scattered in the minds and actions of hundreds of thousands, if not millions, of social participants. No individual or group, elected or otherwise, trustworthy or untrustworthy, can be simultaneously aware of all the circumstances facing a multitude of social actors – hence the repeated popular complaints about the absence of 'joined up' government. The 'telecom system' of the market, by contrast, is continually updated as *every* individual and organisation is both informed by and informs the price system through the choices they make. Even processes based on single-issue direct democracy provide no equivalent to market prices for adjusting to the intensity of different valuations. Here the vote of someone who values a particular good very highly

---

1   Hayek (1948) 'The use of knowledge in society', op. cit.

counts for no more than that of someone else who places the same good much farther down her scale of values.[2]

Employing the 'exit' option in markets also has the advantage of removing the need for agreement by allowing those who dissent from the majority view to follow their own production and consumption ideas without impinging on the ability of those who support the majority position to follow theirs.[3] Markets operate as 'discovery processes' where a wide range of products, organisational cultures and reputations compete simultaneously. In order to be effective, such competition need not be 'perfect' – with large numbers of buyers and sellers, none of whom can affect the prices charged. What is required is for incumbents to be open to challenge *at any time* from new entrants who may offer better opportunities than those currently available. Under such circumstances, markets are likely to generate *more* options from which both producers and consumers can learn than would be the case under a process of participatory democracy. The most that a strictly majoritarian process can do is conduct consecutive experiments in which only one set of options is tried at any time and where those in power exercise monopoly control across a host of policy areas in the period between elections.

Restrictions on minority experimentation brought about by majoritarian practices are particularly significant because the virtues of many innovations are often not immediately recognised

---

2   See, for example, Steele, D. (1992) *From Marx to Mises: Post-Capitalist Society and the Challenge of Economic Calculation*, La Salle, IL: Open Court – especially pp. 316–17.

3   For example, Wohlgemuth, M. (1999) 'Entry barriers in politics: or why politics, like natural monopoly, is not organised as an on-going market process', *Review of Austrian Economics*, 12:175–200. Also, Hayek (1948) 'The meaning of competition', op. cit.

by the majority, but may come to light only when they have been put into *practice* by a minority of pioneers. A large body of pertinent knowledge is tacit and can only be communicated via multiple examples of private action, facilitated by the exercise of exclusive property rights. The latter enables a process of learning by results as people imitate successful courses of action (revealed by the making of profits) and avoid unsuccessful ones, even when the reasons for such failures and successes cannot easily be articulated. Seen in this context, the need to persuade large majorities of citizens/stakeholders *before* any new project is allowed to proceed is likely to stultify the process of social learning and the transmission of new values. Democratic majorities may be in no better position to 'pick winners' than central planners when compared with a system in which multiple property owners compete with one another for custom and patronage and where resources are continually shifted away from those who make relatively less farsighted decisions and towards those who prove themselves better at envisaging the future.[4]

It must be emphasised that this Austrian critique of participatory democracy does not assume that the primary purpose of institutions is to aggregate individual preferences into an 'efficient' social welfare function – a charge levied at neoclassical economics by social democrats who favour 'deliberative' models of democracy.[5] According to the latter, democratic processes should be seen as an alternative arena to markets, where instead of pursuing their own interests people recognise the existence of other

---

4   Ibid. For more on this, see Pennington, M. (2003) 'Hayekian political economy and the limits of deliberative democracy', *Political Studies*, 51(4): 722–39.
5   See, for example, Dryzek, J. (2002) *Deliberative Democracy and Beyond*, Oxford: Oxford University Press.

people's values and preferences and attempt to arrive at a shared conception of the 'common good'. From an Austrian perspective, however, the coordinating properties of markets should not be confused with a narrowly utilitarian procedure for aggregating values into an 'efficient' social outcome. To speak of efficiency is appropriate only in the context of an 'enterprise association' that operates according to a unitary scale of values. The price signals that markets generate, however, facilitate a complex process of mutual adjustment which increases the chance that any one of the *diverse and often incommensurable ends* pursued by market participants may be successfully achieved.

Understood in terms of the need for mutual adjustment, classical liberalism does not reject the notion of the 'common good'. What it does reject, however, is an understanding of the common good as the convergence of diverse goals and values into a 'consensus' position. In a diverse society where there is widespread disagreement on goals and values there is no evidence that such a consensus can be brought about by participation in a democratic forum. Even a society of selfless altruists is unlikely to agree on the goals to which their altruism should be directed. From a classical liberal view, therefore, to resort to democratic procedures *beyond* enforcement of the 'thin' moral rules discussed in Chapter 4 of this paper is more likely to produce conflict between people as they compete to control state power and to impose their own particular values on dissenters.

Social capital and the enabling state: an Austrian critique of 'cultural planning'

Applied to the case for an enabling state these Austrian insights suggest that no matter how inclusive democratic procedures become, it is impossible for the participants in the process to articulate the multiple and shifting trade-offs faced in their daily lives, for minorities to put their ideas into practice, and for the constituents of the common good to be discerned in a collective forum. Faced with a cacophony of conflicting voices, policy-makers lack any equivalent of the price system to enable them to balance the interests of different groups, and in the absence of profit and loss signals cannot evaluate their own successes and failures in matching the pattern of production to the structure of public demand. The problems manifested in health and education systems where market forces are largely suspended, as is the case in the UK, are particularly telling in this regard. Notwithstanding numerous attempts to promote public participation via citizens' panels and focus groups, such systems continue to produce an imbalance between demand and supply. As people have, over recent years, become accustomed to making their own individual price/quality comparisons in markets across a diversity of fields from telecommunications to energy supply, the limited responsiveness of the remaining state preserves of education and healthcare has stood out in increased relief, resulting in a further decline in trust of politicians. In markets, for example, successful enterprises that are 'oversubscribed' tend to expand in response to the profit opportunities that result when demand exceeds supply, or at the very least prompt imitation by those eager to secure a slice of the relevant profits – they tend not to introduce 'interviews' to judge the most 'desirable' consumers or operate strict geographical selection criteria as occurs, for example, under the British system of state schooling.

Tooley and Dixon's detailed comparative analyses of private

and public education provision for the poor in a range of developing countries offer strong support for this thesis.[6] According to Tooley and Dixon, private, for-profit providers of schooling in countries that include Nigeria, Kenya, India and China are trusted to a far greater extent by poor parents than the more lavishly financed state schools that offer 'free' education. Neither does such trust appear unwarranted. The operation of the price mechanism and the spread of reputational brands and 'chain-schools' in even the poorest neighbourhoods have seen private schools produce better examination performance (properly adjusted to account for differences in social class) in English and mathematics, for a fraction of the cost of the public sector equivalent.

Elements of this Austrian critique also apply to proposals for the public funding of voluntary organisations. As we saw earlier, not all types of social capital are equally conducive to the bridging networks necessary for economic success. If public funds are allocated to civil associations politicians will be required either to fund all groups equally – and thereby subsidise practices that may not be conducive to wider social cooperation[7] – or 'pick winners' by offering differential funding according to what they deem the most suitable cultural or associational practices.

There is, however, little reason to believe that cultural interventionism of this genre will be any more effective than its industrial equivalents – politicians may be in no better position to

6   For example, Tooley, J., Dixon, P., Olaniyan, O. (2005) 'Private and public schooling in low-income areas of Lagos State, Nigeria: a census and comparative survey', *International Journal of Educational Research*, 43: 125–46.

7   Arguably, the effect of a highly redistributive welfare state is to encourage the reproduction of such practices. The greater the degree of income redistribution, the less clear will be the signal (not to mention the incentive) to adopt a different set of behavioural norms.

predict which associational practices promote social capital than they are to know which business ventures to sponsor. In addition, however, attempts to engage in cultural planning may stimulate a degree of social conflict similar to or greater than the industrial unrest often associated with industrial policy. If politicians, acting independently or under the pressure of public opinion, offer more funding and support to some groups than to others, then the 'losers' are likely to feel resentment and a sense of distrust. The dangers involved here are all too obvious when the associations involved have a particular ethnic or religious dimension, as witnessed recently in the UK with the tensions prompted by the funding of various 'faith schools'.[8] There is, then, a powerful argument for removing *all* state subsidies to civil associations. Inequalities that emerge between different groups and cultural practices as a result of wider processes of impersonal competition, though not without problems of their own, may be less likely to breed resentment than those resulting from *deliberate* state-sponsored attempts to build the 'right sort' of social capital. Inequalities resulting from impersonal competition also provide a decentralised signalling mechanism indicating which sets of values and practices are conducive to prosperity and social coexistence, and may provide the basis for incremental change via a gradualist process of imitation and adaptation.

If problems of 'cultural planning' are severe in developed nations they are as nothing compared with those in the developing

---

8   We are not arguing here against faith schools per se, but rather highlighting the problems that arise when government funds education via direct taxation in a pluralist society where many parents wish to educate their children in a faith-based context. Religious (and secular) schools based on voluntary contributions, charitable donations and parental fees would almost certainly be a feature of any classical liberal order.

world. From an Austrian perspective, international aid organisations such as the World Bank are unlikely to possess sufficient knowledge of on-the-ground cultural interaction to know which particular groups possess the social norms most conducive to wider cooperative practices. History suggests that the emergence of institutions and cultural norms that promote growth has been largely a matter of accident and incremental evolution rather than deliberate design. In the case of western Europe, for example, in opposition to Karl Polanyi's assertion that the norms of the market were forcibly imposed during the Industrial Revolution,[9] analysis suggests that the rule of law, respect for possessions and the observance of contracts emerged incrementally over hundreds of years of cultural development, providing the background conditions within which a market economy could then take off.[10]

It is precisely because many of these background cultural factors are largely intangible that successful external efforts at promoting economic development are so rare. Attempts to centrally plan the transition to a market economy and liberal democracy are no more likely to succeed than those aimed at planning the results of liberal institutions themselves. Probably the only successful example of a planned transition to a market economy is the case of post-war Japan. Elsewhere, the most beneficial examples of development assistance, such as Marshall Plan aid in post-war Europe, have occurred in countries where market-compatible norms were already an established part of the prevailing culture. This pattern has been repeated in the transition economies of the former Soviet

9   Polanyi (1944) op. cit.
10 MacFarlane, A. (1976) *The Origins of English Individualism*, Cambridge: Cambridge University Press. For a recent survey of the historical evidence on this, see McCloskey, D., Hejeebu, S. (2000) 'The reproving of Karl Polanyi', *Critical Review*, 13: 285–314.

bloc, with the most successful reforms occurring in those societies (Czech Republic, Slovakia, Poland and the Baltic states) where liberal norms were historically established prior to the advent of communist rule.[11]

It is not simply that deliberate attempts to build social capital in developing economies are likely to fail. As the attempt to 'build democracy' in Iraq appears to illustrate, there is also a high probability that such efforts may prevent the emergence of liberal practices by creating conditions within which existing social tensions become more entrenched. In traditional societies, where bonding social capital prevails over bridging social capital and where social rivalries are often based on ethnic or religious lines, any attempt to promote particular associational practices over others may risk precipitating inter-group conflict. Coyne, for example, notes the deleterious effects of development aid in Kenya, where studies suggest that donor assistance has prompted inter-group rivalry by focusing on English-speaking associations in urban areas to the neglect of non-English-speaking groups found predominantly in the countryside.[12] In Somalia, meanwhile, inter-tribal rivalries appear to have intensified in the early 1990s following the involvement of United Nations aid organisations as rival tribes have competed to control the relevant assistance.[13] A similar story could be told with regard to the catalogue of failed development projects right across the African continent, where access to political power has largely been distributed on ethnic and tribal lines

---

11 Boettke, P. (1994) 'The reform trap in economics and politics in the former communist economies', *Journal des Economistes et des Etudes Humaines*, 5(2): 267–93.

12 Coyne, C. (2006) 'Reconstructing weak and failed states', *Journal of Social, Political and Economic Studies*, 31(2): 143–62.

13 Coyne, C. (2006) 'Reconstructing weak and failed states: foreign intervention and the Nirvana Fallacy', *Foreign Policy Analysis*, 2: 343–60.

and where the distribution of aid has become a focal point for often violent conflict.[14] Each of these examples appears to suggest that state-centred engagement in the social capital equivalent of 'picking winners' may be as likely, if not more likely, to retard the development of liberal institutions and bridging social capital as to advance it.

---

14   For a more detailed analysis of these failures see Easterly (2006) op. cit. See also Van de Walle, N. (2001) *African Economies and the Politics of Permanent Crisis, 1979–1999*, Cambridge: Cambridge University Press.

8 SOCIAL CAPITAL AND THE ENABLING STATE: A PUBLIC CHOICE PERSPECTIVE

As we have seen in Chapter 7, the Austrian critique of the 'enabling state' holds even if we assume that policymakers and democratic participants are motivated by a desire to serve the public good. Policy failures are seen as a product of epistemological deficiencies rather than the result of, for example, laziness or bad faith on the part of those involved. From a public choice perspective, however, there are additional reasons to be wary of arguments for state action to promote social capital. If the assumption of public-spirited benevolence is relaxed and it is granted that people are, in part at least, motivated by their own personal interests, then attention should turn to the manner in which institutions operate to channel such motivations.

Economists typically point to the way in which different institutional arrangements affect the *transaction costs* involved in monitoring various social actors and hence the incentive structure that these actors face. Where the costs of monitoring those with whom one wishes to cooperate are low, then shirking and free-riding behaviour are less likely to occur than when these costs are higher.[1] Strong social capital is believed to reduce such transaction costs; the more that social actors trust one another to honour

---

1   Eggertsson, T. (1990) *Economic Behaviour and Institutions*, Cambridge: Cambridge University Press; Eggertsson, T. (2005) *Imperfect Institutions*, Ann Arbor: University of Michigan Press.

agreements and not to shirk in joint endeavours, the less time they will have to spend monitoring each other's performance.[2]

The focus on the role that 'soft' institutional norms such as trust can have on socio-economic performance is an important theoretical insight often neglected by mainstream economists. It does not, however, remove the need to examine how soft norms and conventions interact with the 'hard' institutional rules of society, such as the legal protection of property rights and the formal punishment of acts such as theft and fraud. Trust is more likely to be maintained in an environment where transaction and monitoring costs are themselves lower and hence help to reinforce the propensity for trustworthy conduct. Or, to put the argument differently, trust reduces transaction costs, but placing people in a 'hard' institutional setting where it is more difficult to monitor and to escape the behaviour of those willing to break this trust is unlikely to be a successful strategy in the longer term. It is this insight which lies behind modern public choice theory and which informed David Hume's view that people should be modelled 'as if they are knaves' – not because most people actually are untrustworthy, but because institutional safeguards are needed to stop the few who are 'knaves' from preying on the rest of society. The key question, therefore, is whether institutional incentives reinforce norms of trust, or whether they make it more difficult to detect and to punish untrustworthy conduct and thus remove the incentive to behave in a non-opportunistic vein. It is here that social democratic arguments typically ignore the fact that transaction and monitoring costs are often higher in a public sector setting than in a classical liberal regime of open markets.

---

2   See, for example, Fukuyama, F. (1995) *Trust*, New York: Simon and Schuster.

Public choice theory and the limits of participatory democracy

There are a number of reasons why market processes may be more likely to facilitate and to maintain basic norms of trust and bridging social capital than social democratic alternatives. First, individuals, while never perfectly informed, have strong incentives to acquire information about their buying and selling decisions in markets because these are *decisive* in determining what they receive, with the costs of purchasing errors reflected directly in the net wealth of the individuals concerned.[3] The capacity of market participants to make such decisions effectively is enhanced by the direct character of the feedback that actors derive from the purchase of discrete individual goods or small packages of goods, and hence the relative ease of judging whether or not the product 'works'.[4]

Second, actors in markets have strong incentives to avoid or at least to question irrational prejudices such as ethnic or religious hatred, because the costs of acting in accordance with such

---

3   Buchanan, J. M., Tullock, G. (1962) *The Calculus of Consent*, Ann Arbor: University of Michigan Press. For an update of public choice reasoning in this regard, see Brennan, G., Lomasky, L. (1993) *Democracy and Decision*, Cambridge: Cambridge University Press.

4   This relationship holds for the vast majority of marketed products, but is far less obvious when people make their buying decisions on the basis of political criteria, rather than the direct utility of the good concerned. The proliferation of so-called 'fair trade' products is illustrative of this phenomenon. In such circumstances it is next to impossible for consumers to judge whether the claims of 'reducing poverty' are accurate, or whether (as is more likely) they generate unintended consequences that perpetuate poverty (for example, by attracting more producers into a market where there is already an excess of supply). This may constitute evidence of 'market failure', but seems more illustrative of the problems that arise when people make purchasing decisions according to the often uninformed grand designs that are more typical of their decisions in the voting booth – see the analysis of political ignorance below.

prejudices are borne directly by the actors concerned. Thus, the employer who refuses to hire people owing to their race or sexual orientation and the consumer who refuses to buy products made with 'foreign' labour will pay higher prices than more open-minded people because such prejudicial buying reduces the supply of potential employees or partners to exchange.[5]

In the political process, by contrast, the decision to acquire information and to act rationally rather than out of prejudice has the characteristics of a collective good. An individual's decision to acquire information about the quality of the policies on offer is *not* decisive in determining what they will actually receive. The latter is a function of how the prevailing majority votes. When individual action is not decisive in determining policy outcomes it is rational to be 'ignorant' of political information, an incentive compounded by the high information costs associated with the 'bundle purchase' nature of voting itself.[6] Voters cannot choose between a series of discrete policy options in the way that private agents may 'customise' their purchasing bundles in the market, but must elect politicians who will represent them across the full range of government interventions. The sheer scale of the policy bundles concerned makes it harder for voters to detect which particular policies (such as the effect of trade protection on economic growth, for example) work or fail than for private consumers to judge the merits of marketed products. These problems tend to be magnified by the absence of enforceable

---

5   Caplan, B. (2007) *The Myth of the Rational Voter*, Princeton, NJ: Princeton University Press. See also Becker, G. (1971) *The Economics of Discrimination*, Chicago, IL: University of Chicago Press.

6   Ibid. See also Somin, I. (1998) 'Voter ignorance and the democratic ideal', *Critical Review*, 12(4): 413–58; Pincione, G., Teson, F. (2006) *Rational Choice and Democratic Deliberation*, Cambridge: Cambridge University Press.

contract and tort remedies against deception by politicians of the sort that are available against product manufacturers. Contrary to the 'new' market failure perspective of Stiglitz,[7] problems of asymmetric information tend to be much more pronounced in democratic politics than in markets. As Schumpeter observed:

> The picture of the prettiest girl that ever lived will in the long run prove powerless to maintain the sales of a bad cigarette. There is no equally effective safeguard in the case of political decisions. Many decisions of fateful importance are of a nature that makes it impossible for the public to experiment with them at its leisure and at moderate cost. Even if that is possible, however, judgment is as a rule not so easy to arrive at than [sic] in the case of the cigarette, because effects are less easy to interpret.[8]

In addition to their being rationally ignorant, political actors are also more likely to act on the basis of irrational prejudice than is the case for economic actors in markets. As Caplan has shown, democratic participants have incentives to behave in a 'rationally

7   Stiglitz (1994) op. cit.
8   Schumpeter, J. (1950) *Capitalism, Socialism and Democracy*, New York: Harper and Row, p. 262. Writing in 1950, Schumpeter was, of course, referring to the capacity of cigarette consumers to compare the taste of one brand of tobacco relative to another – he was *not* discussing consumers' capacity to judge the health consequences of smoking cigarettes themselves. Even in the latter situation we posit that Schumpeter's account of the relative ease of making cause and effect associations in markets compared with politics still holds, albeit to a lesser extent. Notwithstanding the activities of the tobacco industry, it is easier for even relatively uneducated consumers to make a judgement about the association between lung cancer and smoking tobacco than it is for relatively uneducated voters to make associations between, say, protectionism and stagnating productivity or between health and safety regulations and unemployment. It is also significant that acts of deception by the tobacco industry have been punished by the courts, whereas the tendency of politicians to be 'economical with the truth' is rarely, if ever, punished in such a way.

irrational' manner. In the public sphere the costs to an individual of maintaining irrational beliefs are trivial because the chance that any individual's policy views may affect the result of an election is vanishingly small. Holding to false beliefs in markets – for example, continuing to believe in the virtues of a loss-making enterprise – has a direct cost to the actor concerned. Market participants pay the costs of holding false beliefs themselves and may profit personally from revising them. In the democratic process, however, the costs of supporting irrational policies are spread across all other voters in the electorate, and since no individual can affect the result there is no personal benefit to be gained from questioning one's support for such policies. The rational questioning of personal beliefs in a democratic setting has collective goods attributes and will, therefore, be 'underproduced' relative to a private market situation. The result is, according to Caplan, the persistence in the public sphere of demonstrably false ideas such as the view that 'immigrants cause unemployment'.[9] Seen in this light, the claim made by social democrats that democratic participation provides a forum in which people can challenge each other's preferences leading to more enlightened policy choices has little theoretical or empirical basis.

Open markets are, of course, subject to inefficiencies associated with externalities and collective goods problems. From a public choice perspective, however, these problems tend to be magnified by political dynamics. In a market, if people are imposing costs on others or are benefiting from services without payment, institutional entrepreneurs have incentives to find ways of eliminating such involuntary transfers over time. A landowner

9   Caplan (2007) op. cit. offers detailed empirical evidence on a range of false beliefs held by voters.

may, for example, introduce fences and install entrance points to the grounds of a park in order to exclude non-payers from the park's aesthetic benefits. Likewise, should technologies develop in the future that enable the 'enclosure' of atmospheric resources, then entrepreneurs will have incentives to define property rights to the air and to charge those who are currently polluting 'for free'. The political process, on the other hand, tends by its very nature to externalise costs by requiring that people pay for 'goods' that they do not themselves demand. Once a majority coalition has been formed, resources can be extracted from those outside the ruling group to pay for the services concerned. Relative to a market situation, therefore, politicians always have incentives to externalise costs – providing benefits to some groups which are paid for by others.[10]

An additional advantage of markets from a public choice perspective is that they maintain the option of individual action to eliminate collective goods problems by preserving the capacity for 'exit'. Shareholders in corporations, for example, often face free-rider problems in disciplining management owing to the fact that the rewards from seeking better company performance are not confined to those who engage in such action but are shared by all other owners. These problems are, however, minimised because individual owners retain the option to sell shares in one company and purchase them in a different and better-managed concern. In the political process, however, exit is *not* an option. The very act of socialising service provision *creates* collective goods problems. 'Consumers', for example, cannot improve the service they get by switching their money from one supplier to another – they must

---

10 Holcombe, R. (2002) 'Political entrepreneurship and the democratic allocation of economic resources', *Review of Austrian Economics*, 15(2): 143–59.

use their collective 'voice'. There are, however, systematic variations in the costs of organising voice for different sorts of groups. In general, it is much easier for smaller groups, and in particular producer interests, to overcome free-rider problems and transaction costs when seeking to organise political campaigns than it is for larger, diffuse groups such as taxpayers and consumers, for whom the costs of identifying free-riding behaviour are often prohibitive.[11]

Public choice analysis does not, it should be emphasised, rule out the possibility that some government action may be required where collective goods problems are of such a magnitude that market solutions may not be forthcoming within an acceptable time frame (there may, for example, be a case for government action to create an emissions trading regime to address CO_2 induced climate change).[12] The prevalence of similar if not more severe problems in the public sector, however, suggests that the burden of proof should be shifted decisively in the direction of those who favour government action.

Social capital and the enabling state: public choice and the corruption of civil society

It should be evident from the above that contemporary strategies

---

11   Ibid.

12   The range of collective goods that only government can supply is in fact much smaller than commonly recognised. For an account of the superiority of private infrastructural provision see, for example, Beito, D., Gordon, P., Tabarrok, A. (2003) *The Voluntary City: Choice, Community and Civil Society*, Ann Arbor: University of Michigan Press. The case for the private supply of many environmental goods is set out in Anderson, T., Leal, D. (2001) *Free Market Environmentalism* (2nd edn), New York: Palgrave.

aimed at promoting social capital, far from providing a cure for existing government failures, may actually spread the disease. Declining participation and the unwillingness of people to challenge irrational beliefs are not the product of undue cynicism on behalf of electorates, but represent a rational response to the fact that participation in decisions about public policy makes virtually no difference to the services that any particular person will receive. Insofar as participation in the electoral process is sustained at all this is largely due to the sense of civic duty that people rightly feel towards the importance of maintaining the democratic process. Political action cannot be reduced purely to self-interested calculation but is informed in part by values and beliefs acquired through the process of socialisation. People may, for example, believe that they should vote in elections because they have been taught at school that the sacrifices in World War II were endured to defend democracy. This cultural attachment to democratic institutions is an important element of social capital, but it is a stock of capital that will not be enhanced by the democratic process itself owing to the incentive structure involved in an institutional environment that removes the 'exit' option.

Participation may be sustained by an appeal to people's sense of civic duty, but even this is likely to decline over time as people come to recognise how ineffectual individual voting is as a method for acquiring the goods and services that improve their quality of life. Moreover, the quality of the participation itself will be very poor, owing to the lack of incentive to become informed. Even a civic-minded individual will not spend much time acquiring and checking political information for the sake of casting an informed vote, since in a large electorate the chance that her particular vote will be decisive in determining the outcome is so small. Such a person may be better off directing her energies to activities that can have a decisive effect on a specific outcome, such as, for example, helping an elderly neighbour. Given this set of incentives and constraints, it is not surprising that voters, *irrespective* of educational achievements and social class, tend to be ignorant of even the most basic political information. In the USA, for example, 70 per cent of voters cannot name either of their state's senators, an average 56 per cent cannot name any congressional candidate in their district – even at the height of an election campaign – and the vast majority cannot estimate the rate of inflation or unemployment to within 5 per cent of their actual levels. Nor can such failings be attributed to the effects of Anglo-American individualism – similar results apply in the case of supposedly more communitarian societies such as France.[13] With rational ignorance of this magnitude, the claim that increased public involvement will somehow improve information and policy outcomes giving rise to greater social capital seems fanciful in the extreme.

The logic of public choice analysis also applies to the proposals for state assistance to voluntary organisations. Given the underlying incentive structure, providing more scope for participation may simply improve access for organised special interests at the expense of the electorate at large. Contrary to Putnam, the level of associational activity per se should not be seen as the best indicator of a healthy democratic order. Rather, it is the nature of the activities that the relevant associations engage in which are at issue. Trade unions, business and professional associations, for example, play a useful role when they solicit voluntary contributions and provide services to their members. It is a different

13 Somin (1998) op. cit.

matter, however, when they pursue subsidies, restrictions on competition and favourable regulations from the state at the expense of consumers and taxpayers, who, being much larger in number and more diverse, find it difficult to organise collectively against such 'rent-seeking'. Where the political process provides opportunities to engage in redistributive or predatory activity, then the impact of a large number of special interest organisations may be to create societies bound up in protectionist regulations and privileges. As a consequence, the number of trade associations often exhibits a negative correlation with economic growth.[14]

In the developing world there is a particular danger that political institutions will be captured by special interests owing to the prevalence of bonding social capital. The existence of strong ties based on kinship, religion or ethnic identity makes it easier for producer groups to overcome collective action problems and to mobilise politically in the pursuit of rents. Relying on strategies of democratic participation may also reinforce ethnic and religious tensions owing to the phenomenon of 'rational irrationality' – if actors can rely on the state to supplement their income then they will be less likely to challenge their own exclusionary prejudices and to reach out to people beyond their own groups in order to generate income via voluntary exchange. Many of the corrupt patron–client relationships that characterise the mercantilist regimes found in much of Africa, Latin America and some of the former socialist countries in eastern Europe are prone to rent-seeking, with contracts and production licences distributed on the basis of kin or religion.[15] To a large extent ethnic and religious

14 The classic analysis of this phenomenon remains Olson, M. (1982) *The Rise and Decline of Nations*, New Haven, CT: Yale University Press.

15 For example, Young, C., Turner, T. (1985) *The Rise and Decline of the Zairian State*,

identification in such societies also forms the basis of ordinary market transactions; in the absence of secure property rights and reputational devices such as credit ratings, people may confine their dealings to extended family members in order to overcome problems arising from a lack of generalised trust.[16] The consequence of such exclusionary action in the market is to limit competition and the gains from trade. Far from undermining these practices, however, state action tends to entrench them because those who prove successful in capturing the political machine can use the governmental apparatus to enforce exclusionary norms via bureaucratic regulation. Protectionist policies based on import substitution and controls on the foreign ownership of enterprises are particularly damaging in this regard. On the one hand, they enrich the dominant familial and ethnic groups that benefit from the restriction of competition, and in so doing tend to encourage inter-ethnic conflict over the relevant distributional gains. And on the other hand, by reducing the penetration of the local market by global brands and management practices, they stifle the exposure of local cultures to a different set of social norms which could lead to the spread of more outward-looking practices and the development of bridging social capital.

Using public money to 'build social capital' may simply spread these public choice problems to civil associations not usually associated with such behaviour. If sports clubs, community groups and charities receive an increasing proportion of their income

Madison: University of Wisconsin Press; Pipes, R. (1974) *Russia under the Old Regime*, New York: Scribner.

16   Grief, A. (1993) 'Contract enforceability and economic institutions in early trade: the Maghribi Traders Coalition', *American Economic Review*, 83(3): 525–48; Rauch, J. (2001) 'Business and social networks in international trade', *Journal of Economic Literature*, 39: 1177–203.

from government then this will change the incentives they face. The defining characteristic of a civil association is that it relies on the consent of its members, who can 'exit' by withdrawing their financial support at any time. Government funding, however, reduces or removes this accountability and creates a new set of collective action problems. In order to express dissatisfaction, citizens cannot withdraw their individual financial support, but must exercise their collective voice as taxpayers. For the reasons discussed above, mobilising a diffuse base of taxpayers is a difficult proposition and puts the general electorate at a structural disadvantage in relation to more readily organised groups. In addition, receipt of funds from government, rather than from a multiplicity of private contributors, makes civil associations dependent on the state and more likely to reflect the agenda of politicians and public bureaucracies. In turn they will be less likely to reflect the desires of the citizens who support their cause.

Experiences from both the developed and the developing world confirm that these public choice insights are more than theoretical speculation. Detailed historical analyses of mutual aid and friendly societies by Green in the UK and Beito in the USA, for example, show that the extension of state provision in health, education and welfare has tended to displace the voluntary sector.[17] In part, this is due to rent-seeking strategies by coalitions of organised producer groups and civil servants to restrict competition. In other circumstances, however, it is the unintended consequence of providing 'free' (i.e. tax-financed) services. When services are provided free at the point of use, those who previously

---

17 Green, D. (1993) *Reinventing Civil Society: The Rediscovery of Welfare without Politics*, London: Institute of Economic Affairs; Beito, D. (2000) *From Mutual Aid to the Welfare State*, Chapel Hill: University of North Carolina Press.

paid a membership contribution to a mutual aid organisation cease to do so. Similarly, if associations can gain government subsidies rather than find innovative ways of generating voluntary contributions they tend to opt for the former and not the latter.[18]

Far from supporting the case for government subsidies, Ostrom's findings suggest that the most successful examples of voluntary action to overcome the problem of managing common pool resources in the developing world have occurred *without* government financial assistance, with the role of the state confined to the provision of dispute resolution mechanisms.[19] As Ostrom puts it, 'If someone else agrees to pay the costs of supplying new institutions then it is difficult to overcome the temptation to free-ride.'[20] Indeed, rather than building social capital, state financing of civil associations often undermines it. When the state intervenes, individuals who do not already have their own institutions in place simply wait for the government to handle their problems. Under these conditions it is pre-existing associations (typically producer coalitions or groups mobilised around ethnicity or religion) with the lowest costs of organisation which tend to capture the state apparatus and to engage in rent-seeking behaviour.

Even when associational activity is not 'crowded out' by state action, the most significant impact of government funding may be on the *character* of civil associations, and in particular the encouragement of rent-seeking in place of voluntary endeavour.[21] In the

---

18　For example, because the organisation only has to market itself to one body (a government bureau) instead of a multiplicity of potential supporters.

19　Ostrom, E. (1990) op. cit.

20　Ibid., p. 213.

21　Although examples of 'crowding out' are common, there is little systematic evidence to indicate that higher levels of government intervention correlate directly

UK, one area where this impact has been pronounced is that of housing. Charitable organisations, and in particular housing associations, are now contracted to build most new 'social housing' stock in a textbook strategy of 'co-production' aimed at boosting social capital. In the process, however, housing associations have been transformed from largely independent charitable bodies responsible for their own revenue and management ethos into an administrative arm of the state. Although housing associations continue to claim that they are 'community-based', as King points out their basis in the community is little more than a rhetorical trope based on the necessity of conforming to government expectations.[22] A similar pattern is evident across many areas of the contemporary welfare state, where charitable organisations

with declines in civil association. Cross-country studies comparing the extent of welfare state provision in Europe with membership of voluntary associations do not find any statistically significant negative correlations – see, for example, Oorschot, W., Arts, W. (2005) 'The social capital of European welfare states: the crowding-out hypothesis revisited', *Journal of European Social Policy*, 15(1): 5–26 (interestingly, though, this particular survey-based study does indicate that individual trustworthiness declines as welfare spending increases). There is, however, a pronounced lack of longitudinal studies of the sort by Beito (2000, op. cit.) that demonstrate the effect of the welfare state in a specific country *over time*. The latter are not subject to the criticisms of the Putnam-style longitudinal studies discussed above. Putnam's data provide aggregate information about trends in the level of civil association on the basis of a selected group of associations. Studies of the Beito variety, by contrast, do not lead to aggregate claims about the overall level of associational activity, but focus on trends in a specific sector (mutual aid) and examine how these change following government intervention. One reason why state intervention may not reduce the extent of civil association is that governments often involve voluntary groups in policymaking and delivery as part of a social-capital-building agenda. It is for this reason that the focus of attention should shift from the volume of associational activity to the effect of state action on the *character* of the activity concerned – and in particular to evidence of a shift towards rent-seeking.

22 King, P. (2006) *Choice and the End of Social Housing*, London: Institute of Economic Affairs.

have been transformed from decentralised bodies accountable to their members to bureaucratic organisations in receipt of monopolistic government contracts. The EU has been particularly active in the funding of supposedly non-governmental civil associations, devoting approximately 10 per cent of its budget to the support of various advocacy groups.[23] Not surprisingly, these groups tend to share a remarkably similar view about the need to extend the EU's powers over such matters as disability law and environmental regulation. In the developing world, meanwhile, NGOs involved in the distribution of aid are frequently 'non-governmental' agencies in name alone, receiving a significant proportion of their funding from tax-financed international aid agencies by way of grants or contracts. As Easterly argues, much of the recent growth in international aid can be attributed to the lobbying behaviour of NGOs that have been transformed from project-specific organisations financed by voluntary contributions to campaigning lobbies demanding an increase in tax-financed aid projects whose goals are so vague that there is little, if any, hope of their being held to account for the successes and failures that result.[24]

The lessons of public choice theory with regard to social capital are straightforward. To recognise that markets, and the interpersonal trust necessary for them to function effectively, require the state to secure a framework of 'hard' institutional rules, such as the enforcement of contracts and the prevention

---

23 Agraa, A. M. (1998) *The European Union: History, Institutions, Economics and Policies*, London: Prentice Hall, p. 319.

24 Easterly (2006) op. cit. – especially ch. 5. For more detailed case studies of some of these processes, see also Gibson, C., Anderson, K., Ostrom, E., Shivakumar, S. (2005) *The Samaritan's Dilemma: The Political Economy of Development Aid*, Oxford: Oxford University Press.

of fraud, is not to imply that state action per se is necessary to promote social capital. On the contrary, extending state provision into those domains where transaction costs are higher than in the private or voluntary sector, and then offering people opportunities to 'participate', is a recipe for undermining social capital or for transforming whatever social capital there is into a resource that facilitates rent-seeking rather than production and voluntary exchange.

9 CONCLUSIONS

This monograph has sought to 'rescue' social capital from the mindset of contemporary social democracy. Judging from much of the literature in this field, recognition of the importance of trust and the capacity for civil association provides new arguments for an interventionist politics. A negative branch of this thesis develops long-standing communitarian suspicions about the corrupting influence of commerce and the need to 'keep markets in their place', while a more positive strain maintains that 'active' or 'enabling' government is necessary to sustain a vibrant civil society and the very foundations of democratic order. Theoretical and empirical analysis, however, offers little or no support to either of these claims. Far from undermining trust, market institutions are capable of generating and sustaining the bridging relationships essential to their functioning. Democratic interventionism, on the other hand, is limited in its capacity to provide the positive and negative feedback mechanisms that are necessary for political actors to prove themselves worthy of whatever trust the public places in them.

The arguments set out here suggest that the maintenance of productive social capital requires that the role of government be confined to the classical liberal functions of providing an institutional framework that protects private property, punishes violations such as theft and fraud, and supplies a relatively minimal set of collective goods where transaction costs in the public sector might be lower than under private alternatives. Paradoxically, the best way of improving trust in the democratic process may be to reduce the number of areas that are subject to democratic interventionism and thus to lower information costs by focusing public attention on a more circumscribed set of issues such as defence and foreign policy which only the state may be able to deal with.

Given the fragile nature of the norms that sustain liberal democracy, any moves in the direction of such a minimalist framework should, however, follow an 'evolutionary' rather than a 'revolutionary' path. Instead of seeking to consciously 'build' social capital anew, the focus of public policy should shift towards a gradualist removal of the institutional obstacles that prevent the spontaneous emergence of trust-promoting norms. In developed nations, where market-compatible norms are fairly well established, this should involve dismantling the monopoly of the state and the extension of competitive market forces and voluntary provision into such domains as healthcare, education and welfare. It does not require a 'blueprint' programme of 'privatisation' and 'selling off the state' but simply requires that services be open to competition from private and voluntary sector providers and that tax-financed agencies should refund those who opt to receive the relevant services from elsewhere. In the case of those collective goods where transaction costs may be judged too high to allow for effective private provision, it is imperative that government action is structured in such a way that it does not thwart the emergence of private or voluntary alternatives. The boundaries of those cases where private property solutions are unlikely to be forthcoming cannot be set in stone, but will shift as technological innovations enhance the scope for decentralised solutions to collective goods problems. The assumption underlying this evolutionary approach is that if government agencies do indeed promote trust and social capital they will be able to survive the ensuing process of competition.

In the context of developing countries, the evidence of the last 50 years offers strong support to the view that states which have pursued relatively more open trading policies on a unilateral basis, and which have not relied on 'development aid' from the international community, have performed better in terms of the reduction of corruption and the adoption of growth-promoting norms. It would seem, therefore, that the best thing for the international community to do is not to construct obstacles that actively *prevent* cultures from evolving towards a more market-oriented path. This requires that developed nations themselves opt for a policy of unilateral trade liberalisation and open borders. Such policies promote greater contacts with the developing world and facilitate a gradualist process of cultural imitation and adaptation as exposure to both business practices and political institutions in liberal market economies can lead to demands for the adoption of culturally sensitive liberalisations in developing economies themselves. Open borders and capital markets also constitute a disciplinary check on the predatory actions of governments by providing an exit route for overtaxed capital and individuals fleeing various forms of ethnic prejudice. It follows that the still largely indiscriminate flow of tax-financed 'development aid' from international organisations should be brought to a halt. Such flows remove the incentive for elites in developing nations to eliminate institutionalised corruption and entrench the destructive and exclusionary species of social capital that sustain rent-seeking and other forms of predatory behaviour.

The overriding lesson to emerge from the twentieth century is that state-sponsored attempts to plan and control the pattern of economic development compare miserably with those that limit the role of government to securing the institutional framework within which individuals and organisations have the freedom to plan for themselves. The analysis presented in these pages suggests that there is no reason to believe that state-sponsored forms of cultural planning aimed at the promotion of social capital will prove any more successful than their industrial equivalents.

ABOUT THE IEA

The Institute is a research and educational charity (No. CC 235 351), limited by guarantee. Its mission is to improve understanding of the fundamental institutions of a free society by analysing and expounding the role of markets in solving economic and social problems.

The IEA achieves its mission by:

- a high-quality publishing programme
- conferences, seminars, lectures and other events
- outreach to school and college students
- brokering media introductions and appearances

The IEA, which was established in 1955 by the late Sir Antony Fisher, is an educational charity, not a political organisation. It is independent of any political party or group and does not carry on activities intended to affect support for any political party or candidate in any election or referendum, or at any other time. It is financed by sales of publications, conference fees and voluntary donations.

In addition to its main series of publications the IEA also publishes a quarterly journal, *Economic Affairs*.

The IEA is aided in its work by a distinguished international Academic Advisory Council and an eminent panel of Honorary Fellows. Together with other academics, they review prospective IEA publications, their comments being passed on anonymously to authors. All IEA papers are therefore subject to the same rigorous independent refereeing process as used by leading academic journals.

IEA publications enjoy widespread classroom use and course adoptions in schools and universities. They are also sold throughout the world and often translated/reprinted.

Since 1974 the IEA has helped to create a worldwide network of 100 similar institutions in over 70 countries. They are all independent but share the IEA's mission.

Views expressed in the IEA's publications are those of the authors, not those of the Institute (which has no corporate view), its Managing Trustees, Academic Advisory Council members or senior staff.

Members of the Institute's Academic Advisory Council, Honorary Fellows, Trustees and Staff are listed on the following page.

The Institute gratefully acknowledges financial support for its publications programme and other work from a generous benefaction by the late Alec and Beryl Warren.

The Institute of Economic Affairs
2 Lord North Street, Westminster, London SW1P 3LB
Tel: 020 7799 8900
Fax: 020 7799 2137
Email: iea@iea.org.uk
Internet: iea.org.uk

Other papers recently published by the IEA include:

WHO, What and Why?
Transnational Government, Legitimacy and the World Health Organization
Roger Scruton
Occasional Paper 113; ISBN 0 255 36487 3; £8.00

The World Turned Rightside Up
A New Trading Agenda for the Age of Globalisation
John C. Hulsman
Occasional Paper 114; ISBN 0 255 36495 4; £8.00

The Representation of Business in English Literature
Introduced and edited by Arthur Pollard
Readings 53; ISBN 0 255 36491 1; £12.00

Anti-Liberalism 2000
The Rise of New Millennium Collectivism
David Henderson
Occasional Paper 115; ISBN 0 255 36497 0; £7.50

Capitalism, Morality and Markets
Brian Griffiths, Robert A. Sirico, Norman Barry & Frank Field
Readings 54; ISBN 0 255 36496 2; £7.50

A Conversation with Harris and Seldon
Ralph Harris & Arthur Seldon
Occasional Paper 116; ISBN 0 255 36498 9; £7.50

Malaria and the DDT Story
Richard Tren & Roger Bate
Occasional Paper 117; ISBN 0 255 36499 7; £10.00

A Plea to Economists Who Favour Liberty: Assist the Everyman
Daniel B. Klein
Occasional Paper 118; ISBN 0 255 36501 2; £10.00

The Changing Fortunes of Economic Liberalism
Yesterday, Today and Tomorrow
David Henderson
Occasional Paper 105 (new edition); ISBN 0 255 36520 9; £12.50

The Global Education Industry
Lessons from Private Education in Developing Countries
James Tooley
Hobart Paper 141 (new edition); ISBN 0 255 36503 9; £12.50

Saving Our Streams
*The Role of the Anglers' Conservation Association in
Protecting English and Welsh Rivers*
Roger Bate
Research Monograph 53; ISBN 0 255 36494 6; £10.00

Better Off Out?
The Benefits or Costs of EU Membership
Brian Hindley & Martin Howe
Occasional Paper 99 (new edition); ISBN 0 255 36502 0; £10.00

Buckingham at 25
Freeing the Universities from State Control
Edited by James Tooley
Readings 55; ISBN 0 255 36512 8; £15.00

Lectures on Regulatory and Competition Policy
Irwin M. Stelzer
Occasional Paper 120; ISBN 0 255 36511 x; £12.50

Misguided Virtue
False Notions of Corporate Social Responsibility
David Henderson
Hobart Paper 142; ISBN 0 255 36510 1; £12.50

HIV and Aids in Schools
The Political Economy of Pressure Groups and Miseducation
Barrie Craven, Pauline Dixon, Gordon Stewart & James Tooley
Occasional Paper 121; ISBN 0 255 36522 5; £10.00

The Road to Serfdom
The Reader's Digest *condensed version*
Friedrich A. Hayek
Occasional Paper 122; ISBN 0 255 36530 6; £7.50

Bastiat's *The Law*
Introduction by Norman Barry
Occasional Paper 123; ISBN 0 255 36509 8; £7.50

A Globalist Manifesto for Public Policy
Charles Calomiris
Occasional Paper 124; ISBN 0 255 36525 X; £7.50

Euthanasia for Death Duties
Putting Inheritance Tax Out of Its Misery
Barry Bracewell-Milnes
Research Monograph 54; ISBN 0 255 36513 6; £10.00

Liberating the Land
The Case for Private Land-use Planning
Mark Pennington
Hobart Paper 143; ISBN 0 255 36508 X; £10.00

IEA Yearbook of Government Performance 2002/2003
Edited by Peter Warburton
Yearbook 1; ISBN 0 255 36532 2; £15.00

Britain's Relative Economic Performance, 1870–1999
Nicholas Crafts
Research Monograph 55; ISBN 0 255 36524 1; £10.00

Should We Have Faith in Central Banks?
Otmar Issing
Occasional Paper 125; ISBN 0 255 36528 4; £7.50

The Dilemma of Democracy
Arthur Seldon
Hobart Paper 136 (reissue); ISBN 0 255 36536 5; £10.00

Capital Controls: a 'Cure' Worse Than the Problem?
Forrest Capie
Research Monograph 56; ISBN 0 255 36506 3; £10.00

The Poverty of 'Development Economics'
Deepak Lal
Hobart Paper 144 (reissue); ISBN 0 255 36519 5; £15.00

Should Britain Join the Euro?
The Chancellor's Five Tests Examined
Patrick Minford
Occasional Paper 126; ISBN 0 255 36527 6; £7.50

Post-Communist Transition: Some Lessons
Leszek Balcerowicz
Occasional Paper 127; ISBN 0 255 36533 0; £7.50

A Tribute to Peter Bauer
John Blundell et al.
Occasional Paper 128; ISBN 0 255 36531 4; £10.00

Employment Tribunals
Their Growth and the Case for Radical Reform
J. R. Shackleton
Hobart Paper 145; ISBN 0 255 36515 2; £10.00

Fifty Economic Fallacies Exposed
Geoffrey E. Wood
Occasional Paper 129; ISBN 0 255 36518 7; £12.50

A Market in Airport Slots

Keith Boyfield (editor), David Starkie, Tom Bass & Barry Humphreys
Readings 56; ISBN 0 255 36505 5; £10.00

Money, Inflation and the Constitutional Position of the Central Bank

Milton Friedman & Charles A. E. Goodhart
Readings 57; ISBN 0 255 36538 1; £10.00

railway.com

Parallels between the Early British Railways and the ICT Revolution
Robert C. B. Miller
Research Monograph 57; ISBN 0 255 36534 9; £12.50

The Regulation of Financial Markets

Edited by Philip Booth & David Currie
Readings 58; ISBN 0 255 36551 9; £12.50

Climate Alarmism Reconsidered

Robert L. Bradley Jr
Hobart Paper 146; ISBN 0 255 36541 1; £12.50

Government Failure: E. G. West on Education

Edited by James Tooley & James Stanfield
Occasional Paper 130; ISBN 0 255 36552 7; £12.50

Corporate Governance: Accountability in the Marketplace

Elaine Sternberg
Second edition
Hobart Paper 147; ISBN 0 255 36542 X; £12.50

The Land Use Planning System

Evaluating Options for Reform
John Corkindale
Hobart Paper 148; ISBN 0 255 36550 0; £10.00

Economy and Virtue
Essays on the Theme of Markets and Morality
Edited by Dennis O'Keeffe
Readings 59; ISBN 0 255 36504 7; £12.50

Free Markets Under Siege
Cartels, Politics and Social Welfare
Richard A. Epstein
Occasional Paper 132; ISBN 0 255 36553 5; £10.00

Unshackling Accountants
D. R. Myddelton
Hobart Paper 149; ISBN 0 255 36559 4; £12.50

The Euro as Politics
Pedro Schwartz
Research Monograph 58; ISBN 0 255 36535 7; £12.50

Pricing Our Roads
Vision and Reality
Stephen Glaister & Daniel J. Graham
Research Monograph 59; ISBN 0 255 36562 4; £10.00

The Role of Business in the Modern World
Progress, Pressures, and Prospects for the Market Economy
David Henderson
Hobart Paper 150; ISBN 0 255 36548 9; £12.50

Public Service Broadcasting Without the BBC?
Alan Peacock
Occasional Paper 133; ISBN 0 255 36565 9; £10.00

The ECB and the Euro: the First Five Years
Otmar Issing
Occasional Paper 134; ISBN 0 255 36555 1; £10.00

Towards a Liberal Utopia?
Edited by Philip Booth
Hobart Paperback 32; ISBN 0 255 36563 2; £15.00

The Way Out of the Pensions Quagmire
Philip Booth & Deborah Cooper
Research Monograph 60; ISBN 0 255 36517 9; £12.50

Black Wednesday
A Re-examination of Britain's Experience in the Exchange Rate Mechanism
Alan Budd
Occasional Paper 135; ISBN 0 255 36566 7; £7.50

Crime: Economic Incentives and Social Networks
Paul Ormerod
Hobart Paper 151; ISBN 0 255 36554 3; £10.00

The Road to Serfdom *with* **The Intellectuals and Socialism**
Friedrich A. Hayek
Occasional Paper 136; ISBN 0 255 36576 4; £10.00

Money and Asset Prices in Boom and Bust
Tim Congdon
Hobart Paper 152; ISBN 0 255 36570 5; £10.00

The Dangers of Bus Re-regulation
and Other Perspectives on Markets in Transport
John Hibbs et al.
Occasional Paper 137; ISBN 0 255 36572 1; £10.00

The New Rural Economy
Change, Dynamism and Government Policy
Berkeley Hill et al.
Occasional Paper 138; ISBN 0 255 36546 2; £15.00

The Benefits of Tax Competition
Richard Teather
Hobart Paper 153; ISBN 0 255 36569 1; £12.50

Wheels of Fortune
Self-funding Infrastructure and the Free Market Case for a Land Tax
Fred Harrison
Hobart Paper 154; ISBN 0 255 36589 6; £12.50

Were 364 Economists All Wrong?
Edited by Philip Booth
Readings 60; ISBN 978 0 255 36588 8; £10.00

Europe After the 'No' Votes
Mapping a New Economic Path
Patrick A. Messerlin
Occasional Paper 139; ISBN 978 0 255 36580 2; £10.00

The Railways, the Market and the Government
John Hibbs et al.
Readings 61; ISBN 978 0 255 36567 3; £12.50

Corruption: The World's Big C
Cases, Causes, Consequences, Cures
Ian Senior
Research Monograph 61; ISBN 978 0 255 36571 0; £12.50

Choice and the End of Social Housing
Peter King
Hobart Paper 155; ISBN 978 0 255 36568 0; £10.00

Sir Humphrey's Legacy
Facing Up to the Cost of Public Sector Pensions
Neil Record
Hobart Paper 156; ISBN 978 0 255 36578 9; £10.00

The Economics of Law
Cento Veljanovski
Second edition
Hobart Paper 157; ISBN 978 0 255 36561 1; £12.50

Living with Leviathan
Public Spending, Taxes and Economic Performance
David B. Smith
Hobart Paper 158; ISBN 978 0 255 36579 6; £12.50

The Vote Motive
Gordon Tullock
New edition
Hobart Paperback 33; ISBN 978 0 255 36577 2; £10.00

Waging the War of Ideas
John Blundell
Third edition
Occasional Paper 131; ISBN 978 0 255 36606 9; £12.50

The War Between the State and the Family
How Government Divides and Impoverishes
Patricia Morgan
Hobart Paper 159; ISBN 978 0 255 36596 3; £10.00

Capitalism – A Condensed Version
Arthur Seldon
Occasional Paper 140; ISBN 978 0 255 36598 7; £7.50

Catholic Social Teaching and the Market Economy
Edited by Philip Booth
Hobart Paperback 34; ISBN 978 0 255 36581 9; £15.00

Adam Smith – A Primer
Eamonn Butler
Occasional Paper 141; ISBN 978 0 255 36608 3; £7.50

Happiness, Economics and Public Policy
Helen Johns & Paul Ormerod
Research Monograph 62; ISBN 978 0 255 36600 7; £10.00

They Meant Well
Government Project Disasters
D. R. Myddelton
Hobart Paper 160; ISBN 978 0 255 36601 4; £12.50

All the listed IEA papers, including those that are out of print, can be downloaded from www.iea.org.uk. Purchases can also be made through the website. To order copies of currently available IEA papers, or to enquire about availability, please contact:

Gazelle
IEA orders
FREEPOST RLYS-EAHU-YSCZ
White Cross Mills
Hightown
Lancaster LA1 4XS

Tel: 01524 68765
Fax: 01524 63232
Email: sales@gazellebooks.co.uk

The IEA also offers a subscription service to its publications. For a single annual payment, currently £42.00 in the UK, you will receive every monograph the IEA publishes during the course of a year and discounts on our extensive back catalogue. For more information, please contact:

Adam Myers
Subscriptions
The Institute of Economic Affairs
2 Lord North Street
London SW1P 3LB

Tel: 020 7799 8920
Fax: 020 7799 2137
Website: www.iea.org.uk